Robert Gordon's College
THE MILITARY TRADITION

Robert Gordon's College

THE MILITARY TRADITION

Daniel W. Montgomery

BLACK & WHITE PUBLISHING

First published 2008
by Black & White Publishing Ltd
29 Ocean Drive, Edinburgh EH6 6JL

1 3 5 7 9 10 8 6 4 2   08 09 10 11 12

ISBN: 978 1 84502 239 6

A CIP catalogue record for this book is available from the British Library.

Typeset by Ellipsis Books Limited, Glasgow

Printed and bound by MPG Books Ltd, Bodmin

ACKNOWLEDGEMENTS

Thanks are due to Jack Webster for allowing the author to expand on notes originally prepared by him for use by Mr Webster in his book *The Auld Hoose*.

Thanks also to Major Maurice Gibson, Regimental Secretary, The Highlanders and to Major (Retd) Malcolm Ross of the Gordon Highlanders Museum for images and information on the links between Robert Gordon's College and the Gordon Highlanders in the years preceding the First World War. David Knight and Duncan Smith of Aberdeen Journals are thanked for information on articles and permission to use photographs contained in Aberdeen Journals publications.

Dr L. J. Collins is thanked for permission to reproduce illustrations in his work, *Cadets and the War 1939–45*. Thanks also to Major (Retd) K. B. Molyneux-Carter of the Cadet Training Centre, Frimley Park, for supplying the extract from the book presented to H.M. The Queen and for background information on the history of the cadet movement contained in his foreword to this book.

Other illustrations are reproduced by permission of Aberdeen City Council, Doug Westland, Michael Davidson (Positive Image), Geoffrey Lee (Planefocus Ltd), and Berry Vissers and Gillian Howie of Squadron Prints Ltd, Arbroath. All the above are thanked for their willing assistance. Individual acknowledgement of the source of each image is given in the list of illustrations.

Particular thanks must go to Mrs Marie Elizabeth Baker, widow of artist Captain Richard Baker of the New Zealand

Shipping Company. Through Don Handley, Chairman of the Durham Association, New Zealand, she has expressed her enthusiasm for the project and has given her permission for a copy of the painting of the incident by her late husband to be used. The original painting hangs in the West Wing corridor and forms part of the College War Memorial. I am also grateful to the New Zealand Archives Office for permission to reproduce the second painting of the incident known to us, by K. T. Russell.

I am grateful to Fiona Reid, Graphic Designer in the Publications Department, for designing the jacket and preparing the illustrated sections and to Lynda Cunningham, School Secretary, for typing lists of Gordonian casualties from the First World War and the Second World War into an Excel spreadsheet where data can be easily manipulated. In a few cases, discrepancies have been noted between College records and information from sources such as the Commonwealth Graves Commission. The author apologizes for apparent errors. Where lines of information are omitted, records are incomplete or it has been impossible to confirm the identity of the individual concerned. Similarly, it is possible that lists in appendices of the Second World War recipients of decorations or, in more recent years, C.C.F. awards, will contain inaccuracies or be incomplete. We would be grateful to hear from readers who may be able to supply accurate or additional information in such cases in order to build an accurate record to be lodged in the College Archives. Unfortunately, information on decorations from the First World War has proved to be insufficient to attempt a complete list of recipients. Decorations do however appear in the First World War casualty lists.

Thanks are also due to Hugh Ouston for his support and encouragement and to Philip Skingley for his time in proofreading the work. From the wider College community, the willing and enthusiastic assistance of John Dow, John Gordon, Alex Urquhart, Dr Bill Fraser, John Runcie, George Watt, Jim

Hamilton, John Souter, Kevin Cowie, Andrew Hopps, Michael Maitland, Arthur Jamieson, Michael Elder, Elaine Brazendale, Penny Hartley and many others in compiling this information and collection of photographs is gratefully acknowledged.

I am indebted to Brigadier Charles Grant O.B.E. for agreeing to write a foreword to this work. He has had a long association with the College (and indeed appears in one of our photographs) and has taken a keen interest both in our history and in our young people.

Apologies are offered to the very many former pupils and cadets whose names do not appear in this work. Many contributors have stressed that their recollections are very personal and that over a period of sixty years of the C.C.F. (and considerably more in the case of chapters on war service) recollections are perhaps not as full as they might be. Samples of nominal rolls of cadets appearing in Appendix E will however give some impression of the extent of involvement over the years. All those who have been associated with the College, past and present, are part of the tradition.

CONTENTS

FOREWORD
Brigadier (Retd) C. S. Grant O.B.E.

It was with considerable pleasure and not a little pride that I accepted the request to write a foreword to this history of military service undertaken by Gordonians and pupils of Robert Gordon's College. Though not a former pupil, I have, particularly in recent years, had a very happy and enjoyable relationship with the College and in particular, the Combined Cadet Force (C.C.F.). This has been both as the Brigade Commander of the 51st Highland Brigade, and subsequently as the Chief Executive of the Reserve Forces' and Cadets' Association. In both these guises, I have been fortunate to witness the excellent work of Robert Gordon's C.C.F.

This book provides a wonderful record of the history and development of the College and particularly the Combined Cadet Force. From its wonderfully remembered nickname, Fort Cumberland, reflecting the school's occupation in 1746 to the services of former pupils in both the First and Second World Wars, it reflects the strength of its continuing military tradition today. It records with pride the sacrifices of those former pupils in all services and arms, but perhaps most significantly in the Gordon Highlanders, and 4th Gordon's with whom the school is so closely associated. Today the school, through the C.C.F., continues to provide the stepping-stone for some pupils into the military. But that of course is not the sole purpose of the C.C.F. Indeed, it has a much wider role which is both to encourage and develop leadership skills, responsibility, self-reliance and resourcefulness in order to develop the citizenship skills of the pupils. It also provides them with a healthy respect for military matters in whatever career they choose to pursue. It would also be remiss of me not to mention the C.C.F. Pipe Band which excels in fostering the traditional music of the Scottish soldier.

This work is a labour of love, which will provide a lasting record reflecting very much the motto "in learning is our strength". It will undoubtedly find favour with former pupils and members of the staff, but it will have a much wider value in setting out the proud record of a Combined Cadet Force, which continues to exhibit and promote those principles of excellence which are so important to society. It has been a pleasure to write this short foreword, and I commend *Robert Gordon's College – The Military Tradition* to the reader.

DEDICATION

Lance Corporal Gordon Campbell, Royal Marines

1978–2006

R.G.C. C.C.F. 1993–97

PREFACE

Robert Gordon's College is a school with long and proud traditions in many areas of its life. The granite buildings in the heart of Aberdeen have seen the inception, development and nurturing of qualities which run from generation to generation as well as qualities within individual young men and women as they grow through the school. One of the strongest traditions in both these senses is the Combined Cadet Force. It has a clear educational remit which supports and enhances the purpose of the school as a whole. It develops qualities of self-belief, self-discipline and self-reliance, as well as the social virtues of dependability, team-working and a sense of identity. It is no surprise that the leading members of the C.C.F. frequently gain scholarships with the armed forces. Nor is it a surprise that nearly all the pupils who join the C.C.F. have their chances of success at University, in employment and throughout life enhanced by their experience.

Both Jack Webster's story of Gordon's *The Auld Hoose* and Brian Lockhart's scholarly history *Robert Gordon's Legacy* echo this view of the significance of the C.C.F. in the life of the school. It is therefore fitting that a companion volume should now be published with the complete story of the Gordon's C.C.F., from its precursor organisations to the present day, set in the context of the service which former pupils have offered to their country in conflict. Daniel Montgomery, current commanding officer of the C.C.F., has brought a typically meticulous and sympathetic approach to the task. Both as a story to be read and as a work of reference, this work has done justice to the Gordonians whose contribution to their school and country he records. It echoes and reinforces the traditions of Robert Gordon's College and it is a matter of personal pride to me that it has been published on my watch.

Hugh Ouston
Head of College

INTRODUCTION

Even the briefest research of materials in the Archives confirms that the College can claim a quite remarkable record of military service, both in time of war and through active participation by both staff and pupils in the Cadet Forces. 2008 marks the 60th anniversary of the founding of the Combined Cadet Force and the centenary of the Reserve Forces and Cadets Association. It also sees the 90th anniversary of the founding of the Royal Air Force, and the centenary of the establishment of the Territorial Army and the Officers' Training Corps in schools of the Royal Air Force, and universities (founded to train officers for the T.A.). Sadly, 1908 falls during the one short period in the history of the College when records are unclear, but there was a rekindling of interest in military activities amongst the senior pupils that year. The first obvious mention in the records of boys from the school being involved in such activities is indeed in 1908, so it may well be accurate to suggest that 2008 is the centenary year of R.G.C. military activity. It is a fortunate coincidence that 2008 was felt to be the appropriate time to hold a reunion of Robert Gordon's College C.C.F. and Pipe Band members. Many of the original 1948 R.G.C. C.C.F. cadets and musicians still have very strong links with the College and it is hoped there will be significant interest in this reunion.

Cadets in 2008 enjoy participation in a dynamic cadet organization with the number of cadets and reservists now exceeding the number of regular servicemen. Cadets are encouraged to make the most of all opportunities, but care is taken to ensure all our young people look beyond the fun and excitement. Our recently adopted motto, "In Learning is our Strength", comes from the former Aberdeen University Air Squadron. This motto has been out of use following the merger of squadrons into the East of Scotland Universities Air Squadron, and is used by us with permission of their Officer Commanding. It highlights the importance of education and understanding. It is also a reminder to staff and cadets alike that although the organization may provide the opportunity for involvement in a fascinating range of enjoyable activities and opportunities for personal development, a balanced and informed grounding in the wider significance of the role of the Armed Forces in society is of greater importance. Regardless of the positions in which our young people may find themselves in their future careers, this knowledge and understanding will stand them in good stead. 1969 stands out as the only year since the Second World War during which no British serviceman has been killed serving his country. Former pupils have been involved in a wide range of military operations throughout this time including in the Falklands, Iraq and Afghanistan. Our cadets are made aware of the fragile peace we all take for granted and of the complex world in which we live. The Ministry of Defence states that:

> The aim of the C.C.F. is to provide a disciplined organization in a school so that pupils may develop powers of leadership by means of training, and develop the qualities of responsibility, self-reliance, resourcefulness, endurance and perseverance and a sense of service to the community. It is firmly believed that the self-confidence and self-discipline required in service life are equally vital to the civil life of the nation.

Pursuing these aims and emphasising the core values of the British Army of selfless commitment, discipline, courage, integrity, loyalty and respect for others form the basis of the training and experience offered to cadets in 2008.

PART ONE

THE EARLY YEARS
AND SERVICE IN WORLD WARS

Chapter One

FORT CUMBERLAND

It is impossible to examine the history of the institution founded by Robert Gordon without becoming immediately aware of strong military connections. Although the purpose of this work is to describe more recent military involvement, it would be difficult to ignore events which overtook the Governors with a military presence quite literally leaving its mark on the school before the Hospital had even opened its doors to the first fourteen boys on 10th July 1750.

The name Fort Cumberland, occasionally used nowadays by staff and pupils in a light-hearted manner, follows the quite unexpected occupation of the school by a garrison of men under William Augustus, Duke of Cumberland, in April 1746.

Marching north in pursuit of a division of the Jacobite army under Lord George Murray, Cumberland entered Aberdeen on 27th February 1746. Prince Charles was reported to be in Inverness and the Hanoverians marched to meet him. On leaving the city it was decided that although Aberdonians had shown Cumberland due hospitality during his stay, there remained the possibility that Jacobite sympathisers might rise in his absence. Two hundred men would remain in the city and suitable accommodation had to be identified. It was convenient for Cumberland that the newly constructed Gordon's Hospital lay empty. The building was inspected by Cumberland and deemed to be ideal for his purposes (although the officers stayed in the more comfortable Provost Skene's House). Trenches were dug, trees removed and the popular bowling green torn up to construct secure defences for the building, renamed Fort Cumberland. A well was sunk. (This well was investigated by a team of boys from the school in 1971 and is the subject of periodic speculation amongst current pupils.) Penny Hartley notes that during digging of the foundations for the new College Library in 1980, a team from the City Archaeology Department uncovered parts of fortifications along with pottery and other items dating from the mid eighteenth century.

The interior of the building fared little better than the surrounding ground, as described by John Mackintosh in the *Gordonian* magazine of December 1945:

> Inside Fort Cumberland the Hanoverian Soldier behaved scurvily. He broke steps and rendered them useless; he badly damaged the capitals and bases of the stone pilasters; he chipped the walls of the staircase; he twisted off locks; he even wrenched doors from their hinges and disposed of them in ways known only to himself. (p.60)

Soldiers of the Hanoverian army returned to Fort Cumberland after their victory at Culloden. Faced with unwanted tenants who had outstayed their welcome and who had behaved in what Jack Webster calls in *A Grain of Truth* a "most despicable manner" (p.76), the Governors became concerned about the condition of the building and were keen to regain control at the earliest opportunity. A document outlining the situation and seeking compensation was drawn up and eventually presented to the King "with respect to the hospital-house and gardens therto belonging, now turned into a fort and laid waste". Only in late summer 1747 was control regained by the Governors who immediately set about returning the building to a habitable condition. The town Council minute of 28th October 1746 records damages of £800 being awarded to the city, of which a proportion went to the Governors of the Hospital towards the necessary work. This is put at £300 by Mackintosh. In his book, *Robert Gordon's Legacy*, Brian Lockhart, with customary precision, gives the exact figure of £259 sterling or 3,019 pounds Scots (p.41). Only after work was completed were the Governors able to admit the first boys and begin the work planned by the founder.

Chapter Two

THE VOLUNTEERS

A century later plans were drawn up nationally which greatly increased military training for boys of school age and would eventually lead to the formation of the modern Territorial Army. A letter from the War Office addressed to the Lords-Lieutenant dated 12th May 1859 proposed that Rifle Volunteer Battalions should be established in their Lieutenancies to boost "the insufficiency of the home defence". It was felt there was a very real threat of invasion from France, and there were very few units of the British Army at home as most were serving in India following the Indian Mutiny. Losses in the Crimean War had also been considerable and the need to boost numbers was recognized. By 1860 a number of schools had founded their own units, which were attached to battalions of the Volunteers. Some school units have been active ever since with no breaks in service. These school units are seen as being directly linked to the C.C.F. of today.

Thirty-seven schools attended when Queen Victoria inspected cadets at Windsor in 1897 and popularity increased. Military training was seen as highly valuable, not only to boost the strength of the Army but also to provide worthwhile activities and opportunities for boys (and only boys), many of whom were living in circumstances of great poverty and deprivation in the overcrowded squalor of nineteenth-century Britain. This was the period of the great expansion of uniformed youth organizations including the Church Lads' Brigade, the Sea Cadet Corps, the Boys' Brigade founded in 1883 and later the Boy Scouts founded in 1908 (by former Charterhouse School cadet and Territorial officer Robert Baden-Powell).

L. J. Collins examines the new movements of the period in his book *Cadets – The Impact of War on the Cadet Movement*:

> Many adults saw the disciplinary methods of the military-based youth organizations as a means of providing a social education: a way of imbibing the working-class boy with middle-class public school values. Certainly the clergy, public school officers and social reformers who took an active interest in the uniformed youth organizations believed that social control through disciplined military training would benefit both the individual and society. (p. 24)

One of the outstanding figures working in the field of social work at this early stage was Miss Octavia Hill (who was well known as one of the driving forces behind the creation of the National Trust). She saw the potential of cadet training to help boys, with "the virtues of order, cleanliness, team work and self-reliance" as her aims. (www.powysarmycadets.org.UK/history.cfm) For the first time, units outside schools known as "open units" were formed, mainly in large cities. School-based units also thrived and by the beginning of the Boer War, almost fifty schools had "Cadet Corps" units, which had much in common with the C.C.F. of today.

Chapter Three

THE TERRITORIAL ARMY

The Territorial Army evolved from the Volunteers in 1908. Public schools and universities were invited by Lord Haldane, Minister for War, to train young men in a new organization to be called the Officers' Training Corps with His Majesty King Edward VII as Colonel in Chief. These men would be the future Territorial officers. It was also envisaged that they would provide a trained pool of officers in case of war. The term "Cadet Force" came into being, with units being administered by the Territorial Army. Eighty-seven schools became involved and formed the Junior Officers' Training Corps.

Other schools formed Volunteer Cadet units at the very beginning of the twentieth century. These units were usually affiliated to local T.A. Regiments. By 1915, ninety-two such school units were in existence and many of them attended annual camps with their "parent" T.A. regiments.

School records do not make it clear how units associated with Gordon's College fit in with national developments of the time. There are however one or two references to military matters. It would appear that there were no formal links with military authorities in 1906, for example, with a request for assistance in providing accommodation being met with some, but not overwhelming, support:

With reference to the approaching visit of the King and Queen in connection with the quarter-centenary celebrations of the University of Aberdeen [an application was received] from the 5th Deeside Volunteer Battalion Gordon Highlanders for duties which the battalion is to be called on to perform on the day of Their Majesties' visit. It was agreed that while it would not be desirable that the College Buildings should be used for the purpose indicated, the use of the covered playsheds might be offered instead. (*Quarterly General Court of the Governors*, 27th August 1906, p. 163)

The September 1908 *Gordonian* (priced 2d) is the very earliest school magazine on record in the College archives. A lengthy article on military matters appears as almost the first item and indicates that military activities were undertaken by our pupils at that time. The writer, identified only as T.B.S.T., describes departing by train from the Schoolhill rail station for camp at Brimmond Hill and gives a full account of a hard but enjoyable camp:

> The question of Territorial camps is at present attracting great attention in this country and it is in the belief that readers of the Gordonian may be interested . . . I want to encourage all Gordonians over seventeen to join the Territorials and have the best summer holiday they could possibly get . . . (pp.3–6)

By 1910, military uniforms were a more usual sight on the Schoolhill site:

> Playground use was agreed to the Territorial Forces Association for the purpose of drill &c on certain specified dates in April and May. (*Meeting of the Governors* 28th March 1910, p. 26)

The *F.P. Association Magazine* of October 1912 (not at that point named the *Gordonian*) introduces the subject of military activities undertaken by boys of the College. An appeal was made for recruits to join the Territorials, and it was hoped that in time a detachment of twelve or so boys would be established.

Training would be provided after school hours if there proved to be sufficient interest. Membership was made to sound attractive, with the prospect of rapid advancement:

> Many fellows are afraid to appear in the uniform, some excusing themselves by saying they have "no leg for the kilt". Let me assure them that the kilt, properly hung, is an article of dress that becomes anyone. To become a Territorial costs nothing. In fact, it is a way of obtaining healthy recreation and holiday. Think the matter over, obey your sense of honour, and join.
>
> If a fellow would consent to remain at school till a little after five on four nights of the week, and to accept the benefits of an interesting course of instruction, in a little over a month he would find himself a Gordon Highlander, and justly proud to be so.
>
> (p. 24)

1913 saw the establishment of E Company, 4th Battalion, Gordon Highlanders, as a Territorial unit within the College. The section soon became an organised half company of two sections and worked alongside two other sections recruited from "Old Boys" of the Boys' Brigade. Boys participated in camps at Potarch, Aboyne and Tain.

Following the 1913 Tain camp, "A Terrier" wrote in the *Gordonian* V5 No. 1, October 1913:

> In the mornings we were awakened by the strains of "Johnny Cope" together with the braying of an ass which grazed nearby and brayed, it was said, regularly every half hour. Later the voices of the earlier birds began to be heard hustling their drowsier companions, while all expressed their discomfort at being aroused with language varying from Latin quotations to that which would have done credit to a Billingsgate fishmonger. (p. 21)

D. Kerrin, class VB, wrote enthusiastically in this magazine of camp routine. Reveille was sounded on the pipes at 05.00 at the beginning of a very long and busy day. Adjutant's parade was followed by drill and only then breakfast. Ammunition was issued and defensive strategies were practised throughout the day. Marching to and from exercises was always to the sound of the pipes. After dinner, "Lights Out" was sounded at 22.15 and thereafter, perhaps unsurprisingly, "not a sound was heard".

Chapter Four

THE FIRST WORLD WAR

Following the outbreak of war, younger boys showed enthu-siasm for military training and, at their request, the College Cadet Corps was formed in order that they might be better prepared for service at the earliest possible opportunity. It is reported in the minute of the Secondary School Committee of December 1914 that 150 boys had enrolled and that "the committee resolved to record their high approbation of the national feeling which had been manifested by teachers and pupils alike". (*General Court*, December 1914, p. 18)

The boys' enthusiasm for training activities was however overtaken by world events and, in what was later described in the *F.P. Association Magazine* of June 1919 as the result of "a wave of patriotism which swept over the country" (p.21), there was a rush to join the regular forces.

As early as December 1914 the Secondary School Committee minute notes that a list was being compiled of former pupils serving in the forces of the Crown. Over 400 former pupils were known to be serving and advertisements were being placed in the press to make the list as complete as possible. Of the 400, thirty were known to have been those who "would in ordinary course have returned to the school after the summer vacation". Interest in producing an accurate document was strong, and by February 1915 names on the Roll had risen to over 700.

Military drill was incorporated as part of the curriculum for the whole school, with instruction carried out by boys from senior classes. There was a feeling of urgency in the classroom in which:

kilt and khaki had ceased to be a matter of surprise, when guns were stacked in a corner to prevent any sort of offensive in school hours . . . Very soon a feeling sprung up amongst the older boys that they ought to be doing something. They were as yet under age, but felt they might be getting ready, and so at their request arose the College Training Corps. They gave up their Saturday forenoons for drill, showing a marvellous aptitude for the work. (*F.P. Association Magazine* No. 2 January 1916, p.18)

Standards were high. Classrooms became "mini arsenals" and the playground "a dusty and dry barrack square". Soon after, a bugle band and signalling section were formed. All boys were keen to progress into the 4th Gordons, and this they succeeded in doing "as soon as they could persuade their parents or could look as big enough" (p.19). It is reported in the article that ". . . every member who could pass the doctor was serving long ago" (p.19). Two boys were "hauled back after they had worn the tartan and earned two days pay" (p.19) when their true age was discovered. With the proximity of the base of the 4th at Woolmanhill, the Territorials had the use of the Schoolhill site for drill practice, and teachers were well used to teaching "with the soft whisper of the sergeant for accompaniment". The rationale behind the training was, perhaps unsurprisingly, thought of in terms still familiar in C.C.F. circles today:

For those who have reached the rank of instructor it provides a character-training which has been rather neglected in our education system. One expects many of the pupils of a secondary school to occupy in later life positions of authority. Yet many may reach such positions without the slightest experience in the management of men. The qualities are the same for drilling a squad of boys, and these qualities are capable of development. (*Gordonian* F.P. *Association Magazine* No. 2 January 1916, p.19)

References to the war in the minutes of the General Court are surprisingly few and generally reflect the extent to which the normal teaching year was disrupted rather than indicate any comment on the war itself. A few examples are given below:

> It was reported that on the outbreak of the war with Germany the School buildings had been, and were still being, utilised as a home for Red Cross Nurses, in respect of whom a payment of 15s per week would be made in name of board and lodging. It was stated that there was a likelihood of the School's being vacated by these nurses . . . before the full School work of the session was commenced. (*General Court*, 25th September, 1914, p. 174)
>
> It was reported that, on the outbreak of war, the College buildings had been utilised for mobilisation purposes by the Territorial Forces (Gordon Highlanders) and that certain expenses had been incurred for cleaning, repairs &c., which would be refunded by the military authorities. (*General Court*, 25th September, 1914, p. 174)
>
> It was reported that the College Messenger, William Anderson, who was a sergeant in the Territorial Forces, had been called for Imperial service on account of the war. It was resolved to recommend that his situation should be open for him on his return. (*General Court*, 25th September 1914, p. 178)

On the departure of one member of staff, Mr Alexander Campbell, to "give his services in the training of machine gunnery" the committee:

> resolved to recommend . . . that any difference between his army pay and his present salary should be made up by the Governors. (*General Court*, 30th October 1914, p. 203)

One item, referring to the circumstances in which one long-serving and respected German member of staff found himself is of particular note:

> ... the committee took into consideration the question of filling up the vacancy created by the resignation of Mr. Trüe, teacher of German ... It was also recommended that, under the special circumstances attending Mr. Trüe's resignation, his salary should be paid up to and including December next. (*General Court*, 30th October 1914, p. 203)

References are also made to work which might be undertaken at the Technical College including the training of munitions workers ("Men over military age and persons otherwise debarred from field service should be considered eligible") and the training of Army cooks. Here it was stated:

> The War Office proposes to place the men on a subsistence allowance of 1s. 9d. per diem, this sum being placed at the disposal of the instructresses ... to provide suitable ingredients for the training of these men. .... Inquiry was also made as to the provision of special instruction of a more advanced character for selected cooks for officers' messes ... (General Court, 29th October 1915, p. 197)

Following Camp at Fort George in 1914, the first boys to have gone through College military training and into the 4th Gordons departed for the First World War. They were mobilised on Schoolhill, quartered in the old Physics Laboratory, and moved south for six months, training in Bedford before sailing from Southampton to Le Havre. Boys considered themselves fortunate to have a Vice President of the Former Pupils' Association, Sgt A.W. Green, as their senior N.C.O. before departing for France.

At training camp in Bedford prior to departure for France, a Former Pupils' Dinner was attended by eighty men (including some Aberdeen University graduate guests) and this proved to be:

> a mile-stone in the history of the Association . . . an unqualified success, and to those of us who were there, and are still spared to us, it lives as a pleasant yet poignant memory. Many dear faces that were laughing round those laden tables are now lost to us, many brilliant careers have been cut short since then, and the world is now poorer by many sterling and brave men. (*F.P. Association Magazine*, June 1919 p.25)

In 1915, the *F.P. Association Magazine* listed the names of just under 900 former pupils in uniform in a quite astonishing range of units. Writer T.B.S.T. describes the fate of many of his friends in the magazine of June 1919:

> Few of us thought, when we looked with respectful awe at the Russian cannon in the Quad, that we would be living in a few years' time in close proximity to other cannon of a very different calibre and potency (p. 17).

Former pupil "F.L.", in the *Gordonian* of June 1917, writes of the war which "seemed to have come like a high explosive shell blowing [Gordonians] to the four corners of the earth" (p. 18) and this is no exaggeration. The list makes fascinating reading and includes:

Private John Abernethy, the 4th Gordons
W. A. Anderson, N.W.R. Rifles, India
Trooper Thomas Barnett, Royal Scots Greys
Captain H. Brian Brooke, British East African Transport Corps
Trooper J. D. Cheyne, Legion of Frontiersmen

Trooper James Cooper, Royal Wellington Mounted Rifles
Private William Cormack, Royal Flying Corps
Private Norman Coutts, Canadian Engineers
Lt W. F. Davidson, H.M.S. *Columbella*
Trumpeter Thomas C. Duguid, Celon Planters' Rifle Corps
William S. Fiddes, Army Veterinary Corps
Private John Fraser, Bengal Mounted Rifles
Harry Nairn, Defence Corps, Hong Kong
James Rennie, Kitchener's Army
Private J. Barr Simm, Malay States Volunteer Rifles
Captain Trail, Wilde's Punjabis
Trooper William Webster, 1st Lovat Scouts.

Casualties

Reading through the lists of casualties in the Roll of Honour in F.P. Association magazines of the war years is a particularly moving experience. It is the personal detail which is particularly striking. In some cases, home addresses or names of parents are given. Occasionally it is clear that two casualties had been brothers. Many facts and figures stand out. There were, for example, 112 Gordonian casualties from the Gordon Highlanders alone. Twenty-four casualties came from the Royal Army Medical Corps, including three recipients of the Military Cross.

Many individuals are mentioned. **Lt Ian C. Fraser** was killed at Loos. A fine athlete and able student, he was described as "an exceptionally gentlemanly fellow". **Captain H.D. Laing** had been in command of the Inverurie Company of the 6th Gordons when war broke out. He had a wide reputation as a marksman, having won many awards in competitions such as the Aberdeen Wapinschaw, which will feature later in this work. He was "a man of sterling character, upright, honourable, fearless, a man whose influence would have told more and more as the years passed". (*Gordonian* June 1916, p. 9) He was killed at Neuve Chapelle.

Sgt Bertram W. Tawse had left his family home at 95 Beaconsfield Place to join the 4th Cameron Highlanders and was killed on 26th September 1915. **Lt Col. John Ellison Macqueen** had been a junior partner in his father's law firm and a major in the Territorials until 1910. He volunteered for service at the beginning of the war and later commanded the 1/6th Battalion of the Gordon Highlanders. He was killed whilst leading his men at the Battle of Loos on 25th September 1915.

Captain Brian Brooke enjoyed the reputation of being a fine poet. He is described as the "veriest stripling" who passed through the gates of the school (*F.P. Magazine* No. 5, June 1917, p.8), but who grew into one who possessed "magnificent courage, manliness of ideal and dauntlessness of spirit" (p.9). The third son of Sir Harry Vesey Brooke K.B.E. and Lady Brooke of Fairley, Countesswells, he had lived a varied and fascinating life before the war. He was devoted to the outdoors, living on the slopes of Benachie in his early life, sleeping in the woods. "His food, for the most part, consisted of what he shot". He spent time travelling the country as a "vagrant piper", and at eighteen settled on land in British East Africa where he worked amongst the Masai as a big game hunter. He returned to England on the death of his distinguished brother, Victoria Cross recipient Captain J. A. O. Brooke, and joined the 2nd Battalion, Gordon Highlanders. At the Battle of Mametz, despite being wounded twice, he continued to lead his men. He suffered a third, fatal wound and died on 24th July 1917. He was described by Field Marshall Douglas Haig as "ever the friend of the ne'er do weel and the misunderstood, the brave son of a brave father" (p. 11). He is buried in Springbank

Cemetery, Aberdeen, alongside his brother. These words from one of his works are quoted in the *F.P. Association Magazine* No. 5, June 1917:

Well, that was the end of it, so ends my story;
One more fellow-sinner has gone to his rest.
I'm not here to paint him with honour and glory;
I know that his life has been wasted at best,
But I really believe that we'll find in the long run,
No matter the length of the race that we ran,
There'll still be a chance for the straight-forward wrong one,
Provided that wrong'un has lived like a man.

Seventeen casualties are named as holders of the Military Cross:

Captain John Allan, Machine Gun Corps
2Lt William Anderson, Gordon Highlanders
Captain Bernard Beveridge, R.A.M.C.
Lt James Booth, Machine Gun Corps
2Lt William Bruce, Royal Engineers
Lt William Dougall, Canadian Expeditionary Force
Captain (The Rev.) John S. Grant, Gordon Highlanders
Major James Henderson, Gordon Highlanders
Captain Adam G. Howitt, East Surrey Regiment
2Lt Donald F Jenkins, Seaforth Highlanders
Captain James McLaggan, R.A.M.C.
2Lt Peter Mitchell, Gordon Highlanders
Captain Herbert Murray, Gordon Highlanders
2Lt Ian Skene, Lancashire Fusiliers
2Lt Francis J. Smith, Gordon Highlanders
Captain David Stephen, R.A.M.C.
2Lt William Sutherland, Gordon Highlanders.

Sgt William Robertson, who died on 14th November 1916, was the son of a Boer War Victoria Cross holder, **Sgt Major W. Robertson** of the Gordon Highlanders. **David Gray**, Dispatch Rider, Royal Engineers, of 50 Springbank Terrace was the first member of the Executive Committee of the F.P. Association to be killed. **Captain William L. Cook**, 4th Gordon Highlanders, had received the Order of St Anne from the Tsar of Russia.

Private Ian M. McLaren, the London Regiment, was killed on 7th October 1916. He had worked in banking and in fruit farming in Los Angeles. He was an enthusiastic mountaineer and founder member of the Scottish Ski Club.

Following engineering work with a Toronto firm, **Captain Hugh Anderson** had joined the Canadian Railway Troops in 1915. He died of wounds on 11th August 1917. **Captain John Black**, King's Own Royal Lancashire Regiment, died on 26th September 1917 at Rouen. He was the son of the Rev. Dr Black, Professor of Humanity, Aberdeen University. He served with his regiment in the South African War and in the First World War in Alexandria and France. **2nd Lt William Diack**, Gordon Highlanders, of 382 Holburn St, had been a reporter with the *Aberdeen Free Press*, showing "great promise and ability". Following his death on 20th September 1917 a fellow officer wrote:

> I need not tell you that we all miss him very deeply indeed. His men were all devoted to him, and we all feel we have lost a friend, whom we respected and loved. (*F.P. Magazine* No. 6, December 1917 p. 8)

Captain Adam G. Howitt M.C. had worked in agriculture in South Africa. He had joined the Cape Town Highlanders and served under General Botha in South West Africa before returning to the U.K. He then joined the East Surrey Regiment, was wounded at the Somme and died on 5th August 1917 driving off a counter attack. His commanding officer wrote:

> I do not hesitate to say that I have lost my best officer. He died fighting to the last – one of the bravest of the brave.
> (*F.P. Association Magazine* December 1917 p. 8)

Signaller Andrew D. Munro, 4th Battalion, Gordon Highlanders, was killed in Flanders on 19th May 1917. He had been recommended for a commission shortly before his death. His family home was at 37 Forest Avenue, Aberdeen. 2nd **Lt Stanley Pilkington,** Royal Flying Corps, of Auckland, New Zealand, was killed in a flying accident on 24th October 1917. **Sgt Arthur Skene,** Gordon Highlanders, died on 6th April 1917. His brother, **Private Peter Skene,** also a Gordonian, was killed on 25th October 1918, only seventeen days before the Armistice was signed.

Lt J. F. Philip, R.N.R., was killed on 18th November 1917 "while on board H.M.S. ————" according to the December 1917 magazine which, with the war still in progress, leaves blank the name of the ship. He had previously been Chief Officer aboard the *John Hardie,* the first of a series of Belgian food relief ships which had sailed from the city of Baltimore. He was "one of the youngest and last sea captains to pass through the Navigation School in Aberdeen" and had served with the Inver Line of Aberdeen, the Anchor Line and the New Zealand S.S. Company "in many seas from the Equator to the Arctic Circle". **Captain Robert Hay Spittal,** Royal Army Medical Corps, had graduated M.B, Ch.B. at Aberdeen University, and was killed after a "brilliant" career. He had served in Serbia, Malta, Egypt and France, and had received the Order of St Sava from Serbia.

Members of the teaching staff had of course also left the College to join the Armed Forces. **Mr Alexander Campbell** of the Junior School joined the Seaforths in Inverness in September 1914. Others included **Mr William Murray** of A. Battery, Aberdeen Section, Royal Field Artillery. **Private James H. Adams** of the German Department joined the 6th Camerons in March 1915 and was reported missing, later confirmed killed, on 25th September of that year. He had joined the teaching staff in November 1913 and had been an extremely popular teacher and colleague. He had written a lengthy and enthusiastic article on his pre-war travels to Germany in the *Gordonian* of June 1914. It was reported to the Secondary School Committee on 5th August 1918 that **Captain Herbert Murray** M.C., M.A. of the Mathematics Department and **Acting Captain John McHardy** of Classics had recently been killed in action. The Principal was directed to express sympathy to the relatives and colleagues of these gentlemen.

Many members of the 4th Gordons found themselves taken prisoner and interned by the Germans. Extracts from the diary of a 4th Gordons prisoner were published in the magazine of August 1916, at least in part to reassure relatives of prisoners that the men were being well treated:

Oct 29, 1915 – Quite well and comfortable if only the old folks knew.

Nov 5 – Letters from home – the first news since September – a great relief.

Nov 7 – There is a theatre in the camp. I am going to-morrow to hear a French play. I know one of the Frenchmen acting in it. In our spare time I am giving him lessons in English, and at the same time learning more French. I think we have landed in one of the best camps in Germany. The General in command is a very fine fellow. He does all he can to help us.

Dec 5 – I wonder if C——— has seen the old folks yet. He
will be able to tell them all about the 25th or part of it . . . I get
a Russian to do my washing for a few coppers. He washes them
far better than I could do, but that means cash from home.

Dec 17 – Parcels arriving in good condition. Swiss bread too.
(p. 25)

The diary tells of the joy of receiving letters and parcels from
home, kind treatment and reasonable living conditions. The
diary owner writes of a visiting American pastor, his membership of a male voice choir, concerts of classical music and a
visit from a Russian choir. He found this music "magnificent
yet sad". Much of the correspondence mentioned in the diary
is from friends and relatives seeking news of those who had
been reported "missing". Only very seldom were prisoners able
to reply with positive news and provide hope that a man might
have survived. The diary extracts end with a note of thanks to
Mrs Ogilvie, Mrs Lyon and the ladies of the Prisoners of War
Bureau for the parcels "so kindly sent".

Meanwhile, following an appeal for a further contribution to
the war effort, 300 boys of fourteen and above undertook
"harvest work" under Mr Peter Smith, Head of Classics, with
classes being suspended for the period of the harvest.

The Otaki Incident

Two memorials stand side by side, with equal prominence,
opposite the College War Memorial in the corridor leading to
the West Wing. One is to the most distinguished former pupil
to die in the service of his country and the other to the youngest.
Archibald Bisset Smith was born in Aberdeen on 19th December

1878. He joined the New Zealand Shipping Company in June 1904 and was appointed Master in 1912. There are many accounts of the incident which saw the sinking of his ship, the Otaki. This is taken from the website www.victoriacross.co.uk:

SMITH, Archibald Bissett. Lieutenant. Royal Naval Reserve. London Gazetted on 24th May, 1919. VC Medal's Custodian is the P. & O. Steam Navigation Company, 79, Pall Mall, London. Born on 19th December 1878 at Cults, Aberdeenshire, Scotland. Drowned on the 10th March 1917, when he went down with his ship, SS Otaki. Memorials on Tower Hill Memorial, London; the Otaki Shield and Travel Scholarship, and at Robert Gordon's College, Aberdeen. Digest of Citation reads: Lieutenant Smith was commanding SS Otaki, when around 2:30pm on 10th March 1917 she was sighted by the German raider, Moewe, in disguise. She was armed with four 5.9 in., one 4.1 in., and 22 pounder guns, and two torpedo tubes. The Otaki had only one 4.7 in. gun for defence purposes. The German ship kept the Otaki under observation for some time before calling upon her to stop. Lieutenant Smith refused and a short engagement of 20 minutes ensued at around 2,000 yards. The Otaki hit the Moewe several times causing severe damage, including a fire which burned for three days. The Otaki, herself, received several casualties and was also burning fiercely. Lieutenant Smith gave the order to abandon ship, but he remained on board and went down with her. The British Colours were still flying. The Germans later described the engagement as, "a duel as gallant as naval history can relate."

Following the incident, Lt Bisset Smith was gazetted Honorary Lieutenant, Royal Naval Reserve, in order that he might qualify for the posthumous award of the Victoria Cross.

William Esson Martin left Aberdeen at the age of fourteen in February 1917 to join the SS Otaki as a midshipman, and was one of six crew who died during the engagement on 10th March. A tribute to him in the *F.P. Association Magazine* of December 1917 reads:

> . . . he leaves the pleasant memory of an upright and honourable lad. One at school who knew him well, writes, "His class-fellows will never forget Martin's kindly personality, his keen sense of justice and honour, his love of the sea, and his great anxiousness to be doing something in his country's time of stress." (p. 9)

The College memorial to William takes the form of the original copy of a particularly poignant letter written by him only two weeks before the sinking of the *Otaki*:

Midland
Grand
London
23rd February 1917

> Dear Anabella
> I am very sorry I had not time to see you before I left but I only got one day's notice. You need not write here for I will be leaving here on Monday or Tuesday. I don't know when I will sail but I am going to the ship about the middle of the week. I will write again and tell you my address. The name of the ship is the "Otaki".
> *Con el amore di un novio.*
> William E. Murray

The William E. Murray Prize is awarded annually to the most distinguished pupil in S3 in English and French. The 2007 recipient was Nikola Tait of class 3S1. She also features as one of the prize-winning Army Section cadets of 2007.

Then, as today, the "ubiquity of the Gordonian is not perhaps so clearly realized" as it is put in an article entitled "The School at War" in *F.P. Magazine* No. 6 of December 1917. There are several mentions of chance meetings of Gordonians in all theatres of the war. "They seemed as ubiquitous as shell-holes and tin-hats" (p.16). An "old Colonel in Gallipoli" is quoted as having said to a new man:

> Scotty, I expect great things of you. During my twenty years out east, of every three trustworthy men I have met, two were Scotchmen; of every three Scotchmen, two were Aberdonians; of every three Aberdonians, two had been at Gordon's College. (p.15)

The F.P. described in this magazine article is reported to have trained at five establishments in England, and at not one of those was he the only Gordonian. At one such school, four of the ten instructors were Gordonians. He met another en route to France, and many more once there. He writes of "pleasant encounters at various points along the line and in many rest billets" at for example the Vimy Ridge, the Messines Ridge, Ecurie, Roclincourt and Ypres.

The final mention is of a "gaily but sadly reminiscent" meeting with four other Gordonians in hospital in England following his admittance in "a more or less fragmentary condition", and he writes of:

> ... happy days, in spite of wounds and scrapes. There we were, five boys of the old school ... mustering among them eight serviceable legs, seven useful arms and nine good eyes. They were all optimists, cheery fellows, doing their work in the spirit of the old school, earnestly, doggedly, with quiet confidence in the ultimate result, and always ready in the rare intervals of leisure to laugh over reminiscences of the school they loved so well. (p.16)

Chapter Five

THE INTER-WAR YEARS

There was extensive debate about the creation and nature of a suitable College memorial following the First World War. The Memorial Tablet in the lower corridor was unveiled by Chairman of the Governors, Lord Provost Meff, on Friday 29th September 1922. As a permanent memorial, the Former Pupils' Association felt that one facility which the school lacked was a playing field. A period of discussion with the Governors followed and a suitable site just off Anderson Drive was identified (after sites at Rubislaw, Old Aberdeen and King's St had been inspected). The Association felt that a playing field would have to be provided by the Governors in due course (and probably sooner rather than later) and that their offer to part-fund the project gave the Governors the opportunity to provide the College with a first-class facility. All members of the Association were invited to contribute and fund-raising was undertaken. A large bazaar was held at the College in June 1923 with sideshows, concerts and fairground attractions. A special "Bazaar Number" of what was by now renamed the *Gordonian* was sold. The field and pavilion at Seafield were finally opened on 18th May 1925 by Sir Francis Grant Ogilvie, the son of the former Headmaster. It was to be a field where boys:

> . . . could meet in friendly rivalry on something like an equal footing. Your association feels that there could be no more fitting and suitable memorial to those who died for King and Country. (*FP Magazine*, December 1921, p. 30)

Following the end of the First World War, great change was felt throughout the regular Armed Forces and cadet movements. There was tremendous pressure on the cadet movements from political and many other sources. In *Cadets – The Impact of War on the Cadet Movement*, L. J. Collins states:

> The political and literary activity [for example *All Quiet on the Western Front* (E. M. Remarque), *Goodbye to All That* (Robert Graves), *Memories of an Infantry Officer* (Siegfried Sassoon)] may not at first appear to be relevant to the future of the cadets, but it voiced many people's reaction to the war, and their hopes for peace: hence the desire of some people in authority to distance themselves from anything military, and this included the Territorial Cadet Force. (p.48)

Following the considerable expansion of cadet units throughout the First World War, financial support was withdrawn in 1923, and units only survived in cases where there was sufficient interest to fund activities on a voluntary basis. Government grants were discontinued for a time and numbers in the Territorial Cadet Force (T.C.F.) units declined rapidly. The British National Cadet Association (B.N.C.A.) was formed to increase the profile of the cadet movement and fight for funding from the government and, in 1932, had gained recognition and the right to run the Cadet Force under the guidance of the Territorial Army Association. O.T.C. units in public schools continued through the inter-war years, however, with their specific purpose of recruiting future officers.

In the 1930s, with rising concern over developments in Germany, units were persuaded to change affiliation from the T.C.F to the O.T.C. Later still, with the O.T.C. seen as unable to provide the numbers of officers who would be needed in case of war, the organizations were renamed Senior Training Corps (university units) and Junior Training Corps (school units). The extent to which Germany and Italy were providing (compulsory) military training for young people was noted and it was clear the UK was far behind. The National Cadet Force (Army), Air Defence Cadet Corps, Air League and Navy League Sea Cadet Corps all greatly increased activity:

> By 1939 there was no pretence that the cadet movement was only providing a disciplined environment where a boy's character could be developed, and where if he so desired, he could pursue his interest in one of the Services. Clearly, efforts to recruit boys with the specific purpose of training them for entry into the Royal Navy, the Army or the Royal Air Force had become of paramount concern. (*Cadets – The Impact of War on the Cadet Movement* p. 60)

A dramatic increase in cadet numbers was seen as war approached. Control of the Army Cadets, Sea Cadets and the newly formed Air Training Corps was assumed by the War Office. A major problem was finding staff to run such organizations. The vast majority of able-bodied men were either serving in the regular forces or found their time completely taken up with duties in the Home Guard or Emergency Services. Working hours had been extended to help with the war effort, and few men had additional time to devote to training cadets.

In preparation for military service, it was deemed desirable that service of one kind or another should be "recommended" to all young people of sixteen and seventeen through the National Advisory Youth Council, with a firm emphasis on membership of a uniformed organization. The rationale behind this was twofold, following the traditions of the cadet organizations. They were to provide pre-service training to future entrants to a branch of the Armed Forces but also provide citizenship training. In *Cadets and the War 1939–45* Collins states:

> The Government was concerned about the lack of welfare and the increasingly disruptive behaviour of some youths . . . The problem was made worse because of the lack of parental supervision due to the demands of war, with fathers away and mothers working shifts in the factories. (p. 2)

There was no shortage of enthusiasm. Boys (and girls) were keen to participate in the training activities and to be seen as "doing their bit for the war effort". The Junior Training Corps existed in many English public schools and many other schools, including R.G.C., became affiliated to other cadet organizations such as the Air Training Corps, the Army Cadet Force and the Sea Cadet Corps. At their peak in 1942, UK cadets would number over half a million, with 80,000 pre-trained young men ready for service in the Armed Forces each year.

Chapter Six

THE SECOND WORLD WAR

The majority of pupils in the present S1 were born in 1995, exactly fifty years after the end of the Second World War. It is natural that our youngest pupils will find it increasingly difficult to relate to a conflict in which even their grandparents may have been too young to play a part. From another point of view, Aberdeen may seem to them to be very far removed from the skies over London in their history books, or from the Normandy beaches of *Saving Private Ryan* and other DVDs in their collections.

Whilst it is true that Aberdeen may have escaped the devastation of the Clydebank Blitz of April 1941, there should be no doubting the profound impact of the war on the city and surrounding area. As stated by Paul Harris in *Aberdeen and the North East at War*:

> . . . the war touched virtually every family in the north east and often most violently and shockingly. Aberdeen itself was the most bombed city in Scotland in terms of the number of attacks mounted over a three year period, and the havoc wrought on Peterhead and Fraserburgh, for towns of their size, was truly terrible." (Introduction)

Following the sinking of the S.S. *Athenia* off the Hebrides within hours of the declaration of war, Aberdeen ships *Rubislaw* and *Ferryhill* were sunk in the North Sea (the latter within sight of Girdleness). The *Royal Oak* was sunk at Scapa Flow with the loss of 800 lives only one month after the outbreak of war. It was clear that with vital shipping lanes, a thriving ship-building industry and busy port all within a few hours' flying time of air bases in Nazi-occupied Norway, the North East would not escape the attention of the Germans. The worst of all the raids was to come on the night of 21st April 1943 when Dornier bombers of Kampf-Geschwader Group 2 were ordered to fly from their Dutch base to Stavanger. They were to refuel and arm and from there to attack the city of Aberdeen:

> As dusk fell in the evening, shortly after nine in the evening, the planes swept in from the north with devastating effect. The Woodside, Hilton, Kittybrewster and George Street areas were particularly badly hit. Middlefield School, Causewayend Church, Carden Place Episcopal Church, the Royal Mental Hospital, the nurses' home and the Gordon Barracks were all bombed and set alight . . . One bomb tore an enormous hole in the front of Causewayend Church. Another dropped in the grounds of Robert Gordon's College and yet another scored a direct hit in George Street. Luckily, in the night nursery next door all children escaped with cuts. (*Aberdeen and the North East at War*, Introduction)

Army units were stationed throughout the city and beyond. The Gordon Highlanders occupied Gordon Barracks at Bridge of Don, the 4th Gordons (Territorials) were at Woolmanhill and other premises included Rose Lane, Fonthill Barracks and the Hardgate.

The large number of military airfields which operated in the North East is quite staggering. Dyce had been established as an airport by Mr E. L. Gander-Dower in 1934, after the local council's declaration of "little faith in the venture" (*Action Stations* p.89). R.A.F. Dyce hosted many units in the course of the war including 603 Sqn with Spitfire aircraft, 145 Sqn and 310 (Czech) Sqn with Hurricanes, 43 Sqn

(Coastal Command) with Blenheims and 248 Sqn with Beaufighters which flew long-range patrols over the North Sea. To the south there were airfields such as East Haven (H.M.S. Pewitt), which was host to 731 Sqn training Deck Landing Control officers and operating aircraft such as the Sea Hurricane, Fulmar and Seafire. R.A.F. Montrose was visited by R.G.C. boys on 17th April 1937 with a report on the interesting day in the June *Gordonian* (p.123). To the north, Peterhead (Longside) was a major base for squadrons including 143 (Spitfire) Sqn and later 65 "East India" (Mustang) Sqn. Slightly further afield, R.A.F. Banff was host to very extensive Flying Training Command operations and the Mosquito Strike Wing of 248 and 333 (Norwegian) Sqns commanded by Group Captain the Honourable Max Aitken (later Lord Beaverbrook).

The Royal Navy also had close links with the city, notably through the "adoption" by the people of Aberdeen of the cruiser H.M.S. *Scylla*. The ship was launched in July 1940 and later led Russian convoys with distinction. At the time of the adoption of the ship in June 1942, generous Aberdonians had raised £3,600,000 against the target of £2,700,000 in Warship Week Appeal (*Aberdeen at War*). The later ship of the same name also had close links with Aberdeen and hit the headlines in 2003 when, after decommissioning, she was sunk off the Cornish coast in a project to create an artificial reef aimed at encouraging marine life.

R.G.C. and the War

Pupils and staff were made aware of the approaching war at an early stage. The well-known meeting of College boys with members of the Hitler Youth organization at Lake Constance during the 1937 trip to Austria comes to mind. In an article covering the trip in the December 1937 magazine, the writer describes a friendly meeting, although it is clear that both groups were aware of possible future events:

> . . . the friendly, overwhelming rush of the German lads round our much smaller party – the songs and the conversation and promises to keep up correspondence – thoughts as to whether these representative lads of two great nations would ever be thrown into the field against each other, or whether we shall all get wiser – feeling that this meeting on the placid water of Lake Constance would never be forgotten . . . (p.177)

In another touching article in the December 1941 Gordonian, Wolfgang Zamory of Class 1VB wrote of having been a witness to events near his home in Germany before the war including activities of the Gestapo, S.S., slogans being daubed on houses and shop windows belonging to Jewish families and, finally, the arrest and transportation of his father to a concentration camp. Wolfgang's father was later released on condition that the family left the country immediately:

> . . . all his possessions were forcibly transferred to the Nazi Government . . . but our town got off lightly compared with some others where the Nazis committed frightful atrocities. I am very glad that I have not to live in Nazi-Germany now, and very thankful to live in Great Britain, especially in Aberdeen, where I have been made to feel so much at home. (p. 209)

Early in the war, a number of physical changes could be seen at the College. Air raid shelters were built under the direction of the City Engineer. (It is reported that during construction, the electrical services cable to the MacRobert Hall was damaged and had to be replaced at a cost of £19 1s.) Shelters were on both sides of the Main Drive and were capable of holding 550 people. This was in addition to the Vaulted Cellars under the

East Wing which were converted into shelters to hold about 200. Periodic air raid drills were introduced. (In the event, there were only two instances recorded of bomb damage caused to the buildings during the war. No structural damage was caused although windows were shattered on each occasion.) Brian Lockhart states that a revised timetable had been introduced with the purpose of ensuring that only 500 pupils would be on the Schoolhill site at any given time. After some practice, all boys could be safely in the shelters in only two minutes twenty seconds (p.195). Janitors, the Master of Works and certain male members of staff attended lectures on Air Raid Precautions and the *Air Raid Precautions Handbook* was issued. Sandbags were used at various locations, and the window of the female teachers' room fitted with steel shutters. This was, however, in order that the room might be used as a First Aid room rather than for the protection of the ladies. The pavilion at the playing field was taken over as First Aid Post. Swimming was suspended because of the inability to heat water due to the rationing of coal. Boys assisted with the filling of sandbags for defence and undertook work at, for example, Forestry Camp (where it is noted that D. F. Law, later killed in action, excelled in sports competition with other participants). Headmaster Mr I. Graham Andrew was quoted in an edition of the Bon Accord of the time (exact date unknown) as saying:

> The scheme as at present formulated would seem to combine a good open-air holiday for boys, with the opportunity of doing work of real national importance.

The article continues:

> The response of the Gordon's College boys is typical of secondary schools throughout Scotland. Since the Headmaster received a circular a week ago, over eighty boys have given their names

and asked for further information . . . Everything is being done to ensure that this "working holiday" will be a real holiday for the boys as well as a national service to the country.

Two Russian cannon had stood in front of the Auld Hoose since 1874. These had been captured at Sebastopol in 1855 and had stood in the Castlegate until 1874 when they were reportedly removed to avoid embarrassing the Russian wife of a visiting royal. The Town Council displayed them discreetly in the front quad of the Hospital, and in June 1940 the Governors suggested the Council might like to remove them for scrap to assist with the war effort.

There are various accounts of war service by former pupils in the *Gordonian*. Air Vice-Marshal George M. Croil, Chief of Staff of the Royal Canadian Air Force, is described as "one of the most prominent soldiers in Canada today". (*Gordonian*, December 1939, p. 56) After leaving the school, he worked on a plantation in Ceylon before returning to Scotland to join the 5th Gordons at the outbreak of the Great War. He later joined the recently formed Royal Flying Corps and was awarded the Air Force Cross and French Croix de Guerre. He saw service in Egypt, acting on several occasions as a pilot for T. E. Lawrence, "Lawrence of Arabia". Between the wars he worked as a fruit farmer and was responsible for drawing up maps of costal areas of parts of Canada. As the Second World War approached, he joined the R.C.A.F. which was becoming "one of the most efficient flying units in the world" and, we are told, "much of its success is due to Croil".

The Rev. T. B. Stewart Thomson M.C., T.D., B.D., Senior Chaplain to the Forces, Scottish Command (R.G.C. 1901–05), writes at some length in the magazine of June 1940 of "The Life of a Gordonian Chaplain in the Army". He describes his many and varied duties:

(The chaplain) is largely responsible for the moral and social welfare of his unit. . . . He gets up concerts, distributes cigarettes and other comforts as well as New Testaments, gives lectures, acts as Sports Officer, conducts classes in French and German, accompanies his men of route marches, field training and night exercises. In fact, he is a regular Pooh-Bah!

Incidentally, it may interest the reader to know that the two senior staff officers in charge of the chaplaincy services in Scotland are both Gordonians. They are the Reverend Ewen MacLean, M.A., Assistant Chaplain-General, and myself. Many of those we help to look after also hail from the old school. (p. 100)

Elsewhere, an unknown writer tells of an incident involving "a Gordonian pilot officer" of a bomber crew returning from a mission:

Having delivered the goods, they turned homewards accompanied by a brilliant display of shells by the Germans. No sooner had this been left behind than a Messerschmidt 109 came up beneath and opened fire, sending tracer shells just in front of the bomber. The ME made three attacks, and only by good evasive action was he left behind. Then a ME 110 came in with a rush from the rear, but the tail gunner opened up and it fled. Almost immediately another ME 110 came in from the front and was met with a burst of fire that plunged him into the sea in flames. The first ME 110 was still making attacks and sending shells, so from 14,000 feet the bomber dived down to almost 1,000 feet and shook him off only to find that a Junkers 88 was now attacking. Here our gunner had again good marksmanship, and the Ju. 88 also went down in flames.

The bomber proceeded homewards handicapped by a damaged engine, but by skilful navigation and piloting the home aerodrome was reached. Such is an actual exciting incident, and a brave one in the life of a Gordonian airman. (*Gordonian* June 1941, p. 173)

Further details of ongoing service given by Gordonians are provided in magazines throughout the war years. A few examples follow:

Capt. Douglas H. Booth (1912–23) is a prisoner in Japanese hands. He is a son of Mr Alex. Booth, for many years a teacher at Gordon's and now Editor of the *Gordonian* and a chief Air Raid Warden. His other sons are also on war service. (*Gordonian*, December 1942, p. 34)

Flight Sgt Edward A. Craighead (1933–39) is another Gordonian who has escaped death by the use of an emergency dingy, and so becomes a member of the "Goldfish Club". He was adrift for six hours on the Atlantic before being rescued. (*Gordonian*, December 1943, p. 88)

Dr David Levack, Senior Vice-President of the Gordonian Association, was granted the Territorial Efficiency Decoration after serving as a Colonel with 51st Division in France.

Capt. Duncan Mowatt, Indian Army, was Mentioned in Dispatches for distinguished service. He had trained as an engineer before working on a tea estate in Assam.

Capt. John Reid of the Hampshire Regiment was wounded in Normandy after completing a six weeks lecturing tour with the Ministry of Information. (*Gordonian*, December 1944, p. 150)

Thomas F. Rennie (1937–43) was with Gordons and Gurkha Rifles at Caluchistan, India Command: his brother, Ian W. Rennie, was Sergeant, R.A.F. Even soldiering with Gurkhas in the N.W. Frontier Province does not fascinate like camping with Gordonians at Finzean.

Scott McK. Sheret (1928–33), cousin of Wing Commander Bader, 116 Westburn Road, recently had a remarkable escape when the under-carriage of his fighter collapsed on landing. (*Gordonian*, December 1945, p. 50)

John Reid, mentioned above, was known as one of the real "characters" of Gordon's staff. He taught at the College from 1948 until 1982 when he retired as Head of Modern Languages. As a lieutenant colonel, he commanded Aberdeen University O.T.C. from 1956 until 1965. He was awarded the T.D. in 1961 for services to the Territorial Army. A keen rugby player, he was captain of the Gordonians team and he was a Past President of the Gordonian Association. John died in April 2008.

1449 Squadron, Air Training Corps

It was through the Royal Air Force that R.G.C. boys first became directly involved in military training during the Second World War. The Air Defence Cadet Corps (A.D.C.C.) had been established in 1938 by the Air League to recruit and train young men in aviation skills. It was set up and run at local level by enthusiastic volunteers following the recognition that there would be a need for skilled aviators given the likelihood that, if war came, the Royal Air Force would play a key role in meeting a very significant threat from the air. As the need for aircrew escalated, and the quality of A.D.C.C. cadets entering the Fleet Air Arm and R.A.F. was recognized, the Corps was asked to train young men already recruited and waiting to enter service. Thousands of well-trained entrants quickly passed through basic training as a result. Activities proved to be very popular. Training included flying, military skills, drill, dress and discipline. Physical fitness activities were promoted and featured P.T., team sports, athletics, route marches, shooting and camping. Active military duties were undertaken and included carrying messages, clerical duties and assisting with moving aircraft and stores.

In 1940 the government formally assumed control of the A.D.C.C. The new organization, to be known as the Air Training Corps, was formally established on the 5th February 1941 by Royal Warrant. Air Commodore John Chamier was the first Commandant and the motto "Venture Adventure" was adopted. It was hoped that large numbers of boys from the North East would volunteer. A target of 800 was set but it was made clear that there would be no limit, should there be a high level of interest.

As a contribution to the war effort, 1449 Squadron, Air Training Corps, was formed at Gordon's College after "energetic action by the Headmaster" (*Gordonian* June 1941, p. 177) in February 1941, only two weeks after the creation of the Air Training Corps nationally. The Commanding Officer was R. M. MacAndrew and the Adjutant James Geals of the Classics Department. Boys joined to do "infantry drills, rythmics and vaulting", and to undertake training in Morse, navigation, aircraft recognition and wireless theory. R. M. MacAndrew wrote in the June 1941 magazine:

> The response of the senior boys was immediate and whole-hearted . . . Offers of services, skilled and varied, poured in. Mr. James Geals (Classics) has carried the corps on his back. By absorbing all Rules and Regulations he has always been a move ahead of any new situation. With Mr. Hector Donaldson (Science) he has fitted up the Morse Room and H.Q. (the long store room at the head of the centre staircase). (p. 177)

An impressive list of the names of fifteen adult staff involved in the venture follows. Mr MacAndrew also records his thanks to the General Purposes Committee for the loan of £10 to purchase initial equipment. He concludes:

> An excellent spirit animates the Corps, and it is determined to make a contribution to the Common Cause that will be worthy of the Auld Hoose.

By June 1941 the strength of the unit stood at 116 boys. Throughout the war years training was undertaken with examinations in aviation subjects featuring frequently, along with courses for cadets and adults on bases across the UK. A very full programme of inspections, parades and lectures on such subjects as meteorology, Morse, theory of flight and navigation provided stimulating training, whilst preparing the boys for possible future service with the R.A.F. The unit enjoyed considerable success. In 1942 R.G.C. won the Browning Navigation Cup. Camps included cross-country, low-level and night flying with practice bomb runs using live weaponry. The training was not without incident. Flying Officer Dickie, attending a course at an Operational Flying School, was involved in no fewer than three forced landings. At Summer Camp 1944, two cadets, A. R. Law and G. L. Steele, were involved in "ditching" following an engine failure. This, it was reported, entitled them to wear the badge of the exclusive "Goldfish Club", membership of which is open only to those who have had to resort to the use of an inflated dinghy to save their lives.

Names accompanying the 1942 photograph of the A.T.C. unit were supplied by John A. Souter (R.G.C. 1940–51), who questions whether the list was published at the time, having been perhaps deemed "classified information". He wonders whether it has, therefore, taken some sixty-five years for the names and the photograph to be reunited. Mr Souter's father, Mr J. A. Souter, is seated front centre (awaiting his commission, which came through shortly thereafter), pictured with other staff and "Dix" the dog, "a great canine pal".

Mr Souter's other contribution, the 1944 photograph, shows J. A. Souter leading A.T.C. cadets back to the College up Schoolhill after the Founder's Day service that year in the then West Church of St Nicholas. Of his father, John says:

> Dad rendered considerable technical and practical expertise to the school over the years and in a variety of ways. Turned out immaculately at all times, his qualities, attainments and conduct were an example to all who knew him. He was very proud that his father was an F.P. (1881–84) as well as himself (1905–10).

The war continued as the initial intake of cadets worked their way through the College. By 1944, six of the original cadet recruits were of an age to volunteer for duty with the R.A.F. and were accepted. The Distinguished Flying Cross was awarded to former cadet Flying Officer J. W. "Sonny" Robb. He is mentioned again in the *Gordonian* of June 1945 when he was welcomed back to Aberdeen "from a P.o.W. camp" (p. 59).

Two cadets, O. N. Edwards and D. Gammack, were chosen to represent the squadron at the Salute the R.A.F. Parade in London on 12th May 1945.

As a fitting tribute to the contribution of Gordonians through the A.T.C., the *Press and Journal* Trophy was awarded to the R.G.C. squadron as the most outstanding squadron in the North East of Scotland in 1944. This followed a competition judging success in all aspects of the squadron's performance including attendance, exam passes, numbers attending camp and numbers joining the services. The record of Proficiency Exam passes placed the squadron "at the forefront of squadrons in Great Britain". With the end of the war and changes in policy for recruitment, it was felt, however, that there was no longer a need for the squadron in R.G.C. The squadron was disbanded on 1st August 1945. J. Geals, Officer Commanding the squadron, wrote in the *Gordonian* of December 1945:

The squadron . . . fulfilled during the war years a most urgent need. Ex-cadets of 1449 Sqn have served their country in many different fields. Many have given distinguished service in the R.A.F. as flying instructors, pilots, navigators, and bomb-aimers, as well as ground staff. This high service, however, was not accomplished without sacrifice.

Many have seen service with the RN, some on special duties. Several were in charge of landing craft on D-Day. We can also boast of service with Air Sea Rescue. Two took special courses in Japanese. One cadet holds the high distinction of becoming one of Britain's famous "Frog Men", and saw service with that branch of the Navy against German defences just before D-Day. Decorations and Mentions in Dispatches also came our way. (p.79)

R.G.C. Army Cadet Force

Meanwhile, a unit of the Army Cadet Force had been established in 1942 under well-known officers from the College staff – Majors Bob Stewart, Sandy Fraser, John Hugelshover (described by Buff Hardie on p. 197 of *The Auld Hoose* as "a gem of a teacher and an absolute gent") and Bob Mowat. Training was at Gordon Barracks, with weekend camps and courses during holidays. Cadets followed a very full programme of training activities designed both to develop character and leadership potential, and to prepare young men for future military service. Drill, shooting, fieldcraft, signals, map and compass work and "living in barracks like a real soldier" were common. The Miniature Rifle Range at the College was opened on Founders Day, 30th April 1943, and greatly increased opportunities for shooting practice. Formal parades included inspections by Lt Col. The Earl of Airlie, Cadet Commandant for Scotland, and H.R.H. The Princess Royal.

At the end of the war there was a fall in enthusiasm. The

unit almost disbanded but was reorganised as a company drawn from 3rd, 4th & 5th year boys in autumn 1945. S2 boys were admitted in spring 1946. *The College Prospectus 1946–47* promotes membership of the Army Cadet Force. All boys are "urged to join as soon as they are fourteen". Membership is seen as important "in the formation of character" but also "should they be called upon at a later stage to enter one or other of the fighting services". In April 1946 members of the A.C.F. attended the National Cadet Rally in London, where the salute was taken by H.R.H. Princess Elizabeth in Hyde Park. In February 1947 the 2nd Platoon was formed, and the Rifle Range brought back into use. Company Shooting Championships were instigated along with a competition with Aberdeen Grammar School. Sgt Watt and other cadets attended a course in "drill, Blanco and boot polish" at the Guards Depot in London.

R.G.C. Casualties

It is recorded that 148 Gordonians died by the end of the war and, once again, the varied service undertaken by Former Pupils is quite staggering. **Captain Eric Charles Middleton** (R.G.C. 1919–22) of the British India Steam Navigation Co. Ltd. is the first casualty to be mentioned in the *Gordonian* of June 1940. He had gained his certificate as Master at the early age of twenty-four and met his death as Master of the S.S. *Parkhill* on November 1939. **Rev. John Douglas Glennie** (R.G.C. 1910–14) died in a military hospital on 30th September 1939, having served in France. He had also served in the University Company of the 4th Gordons in the First World War. He was the son of Mr Charles Glennie, formerly a member of the R.G.C. teaching staff.

2Lt Norman Duncan (R.G.C. 1929–34) had been a medical student at the University of Aberdeen and volunteered for service despite being eligible for exemption because of his chosen career path. He met a nearby platoon commander before an assault. "Norman shook him by the hand and said 'Good-bye'. He seemed to have a premonition of what was coming. A more vital person had never existed. He was always a pillar of strength." (*Gordonian*, December 1941, p. 194)

Ashley Campbell (R.G.C. 1926–36) had been a keen athlete at school before joining the Royal Engineers in September 1939 and later the Royal Air Force. He was the son of Mr George Campbell, 275 Great Western Road, and had been an apprentice compositor in his father's firm of George Cornwall & Sons, Printers, before the war. He was also the uncle of Mr Alistair C. Skene, who maintains contact with the College, and who, as a boy of seven, remembers his uncle's last leave home before his death. Mr Skene's son Iain A. Skene is a Gordonian who left the College in 1989. **L. A. C. Campbell** is buried in Springbank Cemetery, Aberdeen.

Sgt Andrew Caie (R.G.C. 1934–38) had volunteered for the R.A.F. at eighteen. He had been Junior Sports Champion in 1936 and had taken part in a number of operational flights over Germany before his death on 31st May 1942. He is buried in Allenvale cemetery, Aberdeen. Another athlete, **Flying Officer David Cruickshank** (R.G.C. 1918–24) of 81 Cairnfield Place, spent some of his life in Kenya and was involved in flying operations over Germany before being killed in the Middle East on 21st November 1941. He is buried in Halfaya Sollum War Cemetery. **Flt Lt George E. Daniels** (R.G.C. 1927–35) was to have represented Canada in the planned 1940 Olympic Games in Finland had the war not intervened. **Sgt Observer Anthony Mitchell** (R.G.C. 1932–37) died returning from a raid on the French port of Brest on 24th July 1941. His father and two brothers were Gordonians.

2Lt William Martin Moir (R.G.C. 1930–36) died on 4th March 1942 having transferred shortly beforehand from the Yorkshire

Light Infantry to the Burma Rifles. **Sub Lt George C. Morrison** (R.G.C. 1933–36) had served on the *Ark Royal*. **2Lt James Spencer Nairn** had served on the Maginot Line in 1940 with the 51st Division and had been evacuated from Cherbourg. **Lt James Duncan** (R.G.C. 1925–31) had served as Political Officer at Tobruk at the time of the fall of the city. **Captain Charles A. McGregor** (R.G.C. 1925–31) had been Dux of the Classical School and had been a Classics Master at the High School of Dundee. **Plt Off. James A. Manson** (R.G.C. 1934–36) had worked for the Chartered Bank of India before excelling during R.A.F. training and being killed flying a Mustang aircraft over Wiltshire.

Flt Sgt Stanley A. Marr (R.G.C. 1935–38) joined the R.A.F. at sixteen. He had survived being torpedoed twice and had been twice rescued from the sea following incidents while flying. Two Gordonians, **Sgt William B. Barclay** and **Sgt Thomas Breen**, alphabetically the first two Second World War casualties to be buried in Aberdeen, were killed on the same day, 11th December 1942. **John C. Innes** O.B.E. (R.G.C. 1900–06), previously a Member of the International Rubber Regulation Committee in Malaya, was lost at sea en route east "on an important mission at the request of the Government". **William J. Lunan** (R.G.C. 1918–25) served with the Allahaban Bank in Calcutta before receiving a commission with the Gurkha Rifles. He served in Iraq and Basra and died in Karachi on 6th December 1942. **Flt Sgt Norman Mercer** (R.G.C. 1929–35), of 64 Forest Avenue, was involved in the Battle of the Atlantic and in the bombing of the *Bismark*. He had previously survived eighteen hours in a dinghy in mid Atlantic and had also taken part in the "1,000 aircraft" attack on Bremen and Cologne. **Flt Lt James R. Ritchie** (R.G.C. 1919–25) had taught in Egypt. **James Hector Burr**, an Air Raid Patrol Messenger, died at the young age of seventeen in Aberdeen. **Sqn Ldr Douglas P. Fox** D.F.C. & Bar (R.G.C. 1932–38) was Otaki Scholar in 1938 and was killed in June

1943. His brother **John A. A. Fox** (R.G.C. 1930–33) died in November 1942. **Alistair Gove** (R.G.C. 1936–41) was lost on the Destroyer *Mahratta* in the Arctic "defending the largest and most vital convoy yet sent to Russia". Only seventeen of the crew of 237 survived.

Signalman John A. Rose of the Royal Corps of Signals died in the Middle East in 1944. He had been well known through running the Banchory Lodge Hotel along with his mother. His father, **John A. Rose**, who was also a Gordonian, had been killed in action with the Gordon Highlanders in May 1915. This is the one instance which has been noted where a father and son who were both Gordonians were killed. (The hotel was later run by the family of Marcus Jaffray, a C.C.F. cadet in the 1980s.)

Lt William A. Barclay was killed in the autumn of 1944 while acting as a reconnaissance officer in Holland after landing in Normandy on D-Day. **Signalman Lawrence A. Davie** (R.G.C. 1936–39) was killed in Normandy on 7th June, one day after the landings, at twenty-one years of age. He is buried in the Bayeux War Cemetery and his grave has been visited by staff and pupils on the annual Modern Languages Department Easter trip to Brittany and Normandy. His commanding officer wrote:

> He occupied a position of importance and responsibility which he never shirked. His unfailing forthright honesty and straight-ness, and his keen sense of humour endeared him to us all. I made him my confidant, and I liked him immensely for his great dependability. Please God his death will not be in vain. (*Gordonian*, December 1943, p. 147)

Flying Officer Donald Forbes Law (R.G.C. 1930–42), a "most loyal old pupil . . . and sincere friend" (*Gordonian*, June 1945, p. 5) had been the first Warrant Officer of the College Air Training

Corps squadron and captain of the College 1st XV. He died when the Lancaster bomber of which he was captain crashed on 3rd March 1945. His rear gunner wrote: "He was the very best of skippers, and it was his coolness which saved my life. I'll always remember that." Cadets from the College, under Flt Lt J. Geals, acted as escorts at the funeral service and burial in Springbank Cemetery. 1st XV member **Captain Joseph D. Burnett** (R.G.C. 1924–30) had pestered the Recruiting Centre to accept him despite poor eyesight. He was captured after the fall of Singapore and died in a Prisoner of War camp in Thailand in June 1943.

Flt Sgt Navigator Henry M. Bittiner (R.G.C. 1929–39) died on active service on D-Day, 6th June 1944. He was posted missing when the glider in which he was serving, flying paratroopers to Normandy, disappeared without trace, not to be found until twelve months later. He had intended to study Political Economy at Oxford and is remembered for his poetry. These are words from his best-known poem, written at his home at 54 Fonthill Road:

How shall we live,
We, the young, the next generation,
The next inheritors of God's good earth?
Shall we too, as our fore-bears, be afraid?
Desire the past long dead?
Ignore present evil?
Benumb our minds against the future,
Which lies alone in our two hands?

You might have liked us.
Of course, you've seen us,
Laughing in the dawning by the shore,
Lying in the hot sun at noon-day,
Loving and caressing at eventide,
And yet you know us not.

Robert Gordon's College Section, "E" Company, 4th. Gordons in *The Gordonian* 1919

Sample advertisement of local interest in F.P. Association magazine during the war years

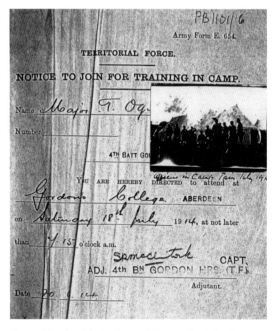

Camp Warning Notice June 1914 issued to Maj. T Ogilvie who later commanded the Battalion and was appointed to the office of the C.M.G.
Photograph: Gordon Highlanders Museum

4th. Gordons in France during W.W.1

Gordonians, E. Company, 4th. Gordons at Camp at Tain, summer 1913

Below: Sinking of the SS "Otaki" by the German Raider "Moewe" by K. T. Russell circa 1917

By permission of Archives New Zealand/Te Rua Mahara o te Kāwanatanga Wellington Office [Archives Reference: AAAC 898 NCWA Q200]

Lt. Col. John E. MacQueen, 6th Battalion Gordon Highlanders. Killed 25th September 1915

Capt. Brian Brooke, 2nd Battalion Gordon Highlanders. Killed 24th July 1917

R.G.C. boys with members of Hitler Youth at Lake Constance during a trip to Austria 1937

R.G.C. boys assist with the harvest
Bon Accord Magazine, in The Gordonian December 1939

Construction of College Air Raid Shelters September 1939. *Photograph: Aberdeen Journals Ltd.*

R.G.C. boys filling sandbags at Aberdeen Harbour, 4th September 1939. *Photograph: Aberdeen Journals Ltd*

Removal of cannon from Front Quad
Photograph: Aberdeen Journals Ltd.

R.G.C. boys undertake work at Forestry Camp, 1941
Bon Accord Magazine, in The Gordonian, December 1941

ROLL OF SERVICE

Anderson, James A. (1934-8), "Rothley," Bieldside—Driver, R.A.S.C.
Anderson, John N. (1930-37), 84 Anderson Drive South—Sapper, R.E.
Anderson, Douglas A. (1931-5), 51 Cranford Road—Signalman, R.C. of S.
Anderson, Ronald (1913-18), M.B.Ch.B., Brixton Road, London—M.O., A.R.P.
Allan, James (1912-18), Kemnay—Forester, Timber Control.
Auld, James D. (1896-7), Holland Park, London—Paymaster Commander, R.N.R.
Angus, William C. (1921-7), "Chislehurst," Cults—Private, R.A.O.C.
Ames, Joseph B. A. (1931-9), Bucksburn—Signalman, Div. Signals.
Angus, Douglas J. (1935-8), Morningside Road—Gunner, R.A.
Angus, Alexr. R. (1934-7), Morningside Road—Bdr. Surv., R.A.   Killed in Action.
Angus, John (1929-35), "Chislehurst, Cults—2nd Lt., Gordon Highlanders.
Appleton, Frederick W. (1924-7), 38 Menzies Road—Cpl., A.A. Signals.
Arthur, John H. (1929-30), 368 King Street—A/Cpl. R.A.F.
Anderson, Robert (1930-5), Police Station, Peterculter—Signalman, R.C. of S.
Anderson, Eric W. (1928-37), Hotel, Tomintoul—L.A.C., R.A.F.
Annand, James (1929-36), 580 King Street—Bdr., R.A.
Angus, James A. (1928-35), 8 Ferryhill Terrace—Signalman, Div. Signals.
Allan, Edwin (1930-1), 14 Esslemont Avenue—L-Cpl., Gordon Highlanders.
Arklay, Richard L. (1933-6), King Edward, Banff—Apprentice, M.N.
Angus, William R. (1929-32), Malvern Drive, Ilford—Signalman, R.C. of S.
Argo, Alan B. (1931-4), 16 Wallfield Place—Bdr., R.A.
Auld, Joseph J. (1929-35), 1 Morningside Road—Sgt., R.A.M.C.
Anderson, William A. (1917-24), 6 Ferryhill Place—Sgt., R.A.M.C.
Adams, William J. (1931-5), 21 Jasmine Terrace—W/O, R.A.F.
Anderson, John (1924-8), C.A., Banff—2nd Lt., Gordon Highlanders.
Anderson, Robert (1931-4), Balmedie Village—Cpl., R.A.F.
Archibald, Thomas C. (1927-32), 8 Harcourt Road—Pte., R.C. of S.
Allan, David R. (1929-31), Ornside, Muir-of-Ord—A/C2, R.A.F.
Allan, Duncan (1921-6), 26 Hilton Place—Capt., R.A.
Allan, Robert F. (1917-21), South Africa—Capt., Royal East African Pay Corps.
Allan, James (1920-25)   —Lieut. Commander, R.N.
Anderson, Henry J. P. (1889-1897), M.A., O.B.E., China-Hong Kong British
   Publicity Committee.
Brown, William J. (1926-32), 12 Holburn Road—2nd Lt., R.A.
Bruce, Alexander (1921-7), 46 Bedford Place—Capt., Gordon Highlanders.
Booth, George (1929-36), Muchalls—Signalman, R.C. of S.
Beaton, Walter W. (1933-35), Westburn Crescent—L/Bdr., R.A.
Burns, Andrew S. (1912-14), M.B.Ch.B., Uxbridge—Squadron Leader, R.A.F.
Burgess, Douglas C. (1930-6), 37 Great Northern Rd.—Signalman, R.C. of S.
Blacklaw, James S. (1931-5), Abbotswell Road—L/Cpl., R.A.M.C.
Barr, John D. (1927-34), 16 Brimmond Place—E.R.A., R.N.
Boyd, Gordon (1929-37), 201 King Street—Pte., R.A.O.C.
Bothwell, William M. (1930-1), Muirtack Schoolhouse, Ellon—Pte., A. & S. Hrs.
Buchan, Charles M. (1930-37), 4 Cattofield Place—Signalman, R.C. of S.
Booth, John B. (1934-6), Banchory—Signalman, R.C. of S.
Blacklaws, Alexr. (1929-31), "Ashvale," Stonehaven—Gunner, R.A.
Bruce, Norman A. (1935-6), 146 Osborne Place—Apprentice Fitter, Marine Engineer-
   ing to Admiralty.
Barry, Brodie (1930-33), 96 Bon-Accord Street—Signalman, R.C. of S.
Burnett, Alastair S. M. (1931-33), 21 Richmond Street—A/C2, R.A.F.
Blacklaw, James S. (1931-35), M.M., "Jesmond," Abbotswell Rd.—Cpl., R.A.M.C.

"Roll of Service"
Page 1 (of 15) in
The Gordonian,
December 1940

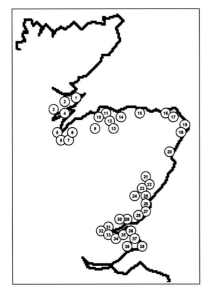

W.W.11 Military Airfields in the North East of Scotland

1	Fearn	21	Fordoun
2	Evanton	22	Edzell
3	Alness	23	Kinnell
4	Black Isle	24	Stracathro
5	Longman (Inverness)	25	Montrose
6	Leanach	26	Buddon
7	Brackla	27	Arbroath
8	Dalcross (Inverness)	28	East Haven
9	Forres	29	Dundee
10	Kinloss	30	Whitefield
11	Lossiemouth	31	Perth
12	Milltown	32	Methven
13	Elgin	33	Findo Gask
14	Dallachy	34	Buttergask
15	Banff (Boyndie)	35	Stravithie
16	Fraserburgh	36	Woodhaven
17	Rattray (Crimmond)	37	Leuchars
18	Peterhead	38	Crail
19	Longside	39	Dunino
20	Dyce (Aberdeen)		

Founder's Day procession 1941
Bon Accord Magazine in The Gordonian
December 1941

By Appointment to King George VI.

STILL
AT YOUR SERVICE
In Spite of Difficulties

Quality Goods
for Your Table

MITCHELL & MUIL
— LTD. —

Shops and Vans throughout the City

RESTAURANTS:

25 UNION STREET. | THE ST. NICHOLAS CAFÉ.
STONEHAVEN CAFÉ. | THE WEST END CAFÉ Ltd.

AND NOW

THE CAPITOL CAFÉ, Union Street.

Advertisement for well-known local business Mitchell & Muil in *The Gordonian* June 1942

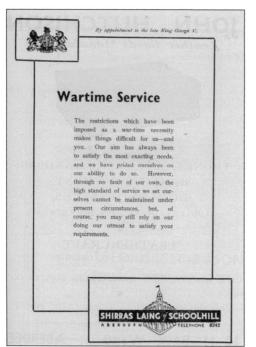

Wartime Service

The restrictions which have been imposed as a war-time necessity makes things difficult for us—and you. Our aim has always been to satisfy the most exacting needs, and we have prided ourselves on our ability to do so. However, through no fault of our own, the high standard of service we set ourselves cannot be maintained under present circumstances, but, of course, you may still rely on our doing our utmost to satisfy your requirements.

By appointment to the late King George V.

SHIRRAS LAING of SCHOOLHILL
ABERDEEN   TELEPHONE 8242

Advertisement for well-known local business Shirras Laing of Schoolhill in *The Gordonian* December 1942

Service
ALL THROUGH
OUR DEPARTMENTS

Not so easy to give you our usual good SERVICE under war-time conditions, but we do our best to be helpful.

RAINWEAR DEPT.   FANCY GOODS DEPT.

SPORTS DEPT.   TRAVELWARE DEPT.   TOY DEPT.

THE RUBBER SHOP
10-18 ST NICHOLAS STREET · ABERDEEN

Advertisement for well-known local business the Rubber Shop in *The Gordonian* June 1943

Poster advertising Air Training Corps membership and training
Air Cadet Gazette, 1943, in Cadets and the War 1939-45, L.J. Collins, Jade Publishing Ltd., 2005.

Poster promoting training through the Army Cadet Force. *WO Technical Training in the A.C.F., 1945, in Cadets and the War 1939-45, L.J. Collins, Jade Publishing Ltd., 2005*

1449 Squadron, Air Training Corps, in front of the Auld Hoose 1941

Back Row (L to R): R. Duncan, H.P. Robb, C.G. MacLean, C.B. Milne, W.C. Todd, P.M. Mitchell, G.A. Williamson, G.I. Milne, A.W. Nicholson, A. Tullett, A.D. Reid, W.T.D. Copland, G.F. Rainnie, J.M. Thomson, I. Elder, W.F. Williamson, L.J.S.E. Jaffrey
4th Row (L to R): T. Henry, R.P. Sutherland, I.A. Thomson, I.M. Mackay, G. Stuart, T.A. Fleming, D.A. Hardie, R.G. Farquhar, I.W. Minto, W. Alexander, H.R. Cooper, G.A. Sinclair, E.G. Cowieson, J.A. Low, D.K. Farquharson, K.R. Main, J.H. Watson, G.D.H. Watt
3rd Row (L to R): W.A. Lamb, G. Nicholson, D.L. Robertson, J. Brown, G.W. Ross, N.I. MacInnes, W. Youngson, H. Strachan, D.R. Ewen, R.G. Giuliani, A. Shirreffs, I.D. Ewen, C.A. Massie, G. Coutts, J.M. Brown, J.M. Caldwell
2nd Row (L to R): J.C. Shearer, S.A. Lamb, W.J. Taylor, A. Gardner, G. Garrow, J. Cowie,
R. Patrick, J.W. Wright, J.D.M. Marriott, A. Walden, A.G. Chisholm,
E.A. Anderson, A. Leckie, A.A.C. Crombie, R. Cattanach
Front Row (L to R): S.A. Troup; Sgt R. Adams; Captain Watt (ex Mercantile Marine); D.F. Law (W.O.); F/O G.B. Dickie (ex 5th Gordons); F/Lt R.M. MacAndrew* (ex RAF) – O.C.; I.G. Andrew* (Headmaster); F/O J. Geals* - ADJT.; F/O H.A. Donaldson*; Mr J.A. Souter*; Mr W.J. Cantlay (ex RAF); Sgt K.G.A. Taylor; "Dix" (Mascot) – Dog owned by F/O G.B. Dickie.
Absent: Mr J. Gordon* (ex Royal Scots); Lt H.T. Shirley* (ex H.L.I.); I.M. Forbes, W. Sutherland, J.R. Wood
Cadets: Taylor, Sutherland, Fleming, C.B. Milne to Sgt, Coutts, Rainnie, G.A. Williamson to CPL, Cooper, Gardner to CPL at H.Q. (Admin)
* Denotes members of school staff

A.T.C. cadets returning from 1944 Founder's Day service in the West Church of St. Nicholas led by J.A. Souter

PRO PATRIA

Sergeant-Observer
William B. Barclay
(1934-37), R.A.F.

Pilot Officer
George A. Bisset
(1920-23), R.A.F.V.R.

Sergeant-Observer
Thomas D. Breen
(1935-40), R.A.F.

Sergeant
Alexander B. Cowie
(1935-37), R.A.F.

Sapper
Malcolm C. Duncan
(1933-35), R.E.

Pilot Officer
Charles W. G. Gray
(1928-33), R.A.F.

Flight Engineer
George Green
(1935-37), Bomber Com.

Pilot Officer
James A. Manson
(1934-36), R.A.F.

Flight-Sergeant
Norman A. Mercer
(1929-35), R.A.F.

Signalman
Nelson D. Ogg
(1932-35), R.C. of S.

Pilot Officer
William F. Raffan
(1930-33), R.A.F.

Sergeant Radio Observer
James S. Salmond
(1925-30).

Pro Patria. One of many such pages which appeared in *The Gordonian* throughout the war years

Army cadets on Schoolhill circa 1944

PRO PATRIA

Messenger
James H. Burr
(1938-42), A.R.P.

Gordonian tribute to James H. Burr, Air Raid Precautions messenger killed in Hilton Drive, 21st April 1943

Article in the Berliner Illustrierte Zeitung depicting the 1943 air raid on Aberdeen
In Aberdeen and the North East at War, P Harris, Lomond Books 1995

Weapon training, Cultybraggan, 1950s
Left to right: C.S.M. Ian Mennie, Pipe Major Kenneth Melvin, Drum Sgt. John
Runcie, Inspecting Officer Capt. Oliver McLaughlan, Sgt. G. Westwood, Cpl. Alan
Simpson, Alex Urquhart, Leslie Innes, Brian McCulloch

Cadets depart for camp at Strensall, Yorkshire, 1954
Cadets include (left to right) John Allan, Bill Fraser, Tommy Deans, Alex Urquhart, Ian Jolly, Bill Brandie, Alfred Cruickshank, Ivor Allan, GW Whyte, Russell Martin, Ian Wildgoose, Hugh Rennie & Harvey Pole
Photograph: Aberdeen Journals Ltd.

Post-war photograph of R.G.C. Army Cadet Force (June 1947)

Far left: Tom Collins, John Gordon & John Dow, Etchachan 1950s

Left: Ian Mennie, George Watt and Robin McLaughlin on Union St. April 1952. Note the .303 rifles!

Buddon Camp 1952. *Photograph submitted by George Watt, second from left*

John Gordon and Ron Glasgow with cadets, Loch Builg, circa 1959

Cadets parade through Comrie whilst at Cultybraggan Camp 1950s. Front rank includes George Watt and Jimmy Pringle

ROBERT GORDON'S COLLEGE

COMMANDING OFFICERS

1941
Air Training Corps

Fl.Lt. R.M McAndrew — 1943
Fl.Lt. J. Geals — 1945

1942
Army Cadet Force

Maj. R.R. Stewart — 1944
Cap. A.S. Fraser — 1945
Maj. J.B. Hugelshofer — 1946
Maj. R.P. Mowat — 1948

1948
Combined Cadet Force

Maj. M.M. MacRae — 1952
Capt. O.W McLaughlan — 1953
Capt. R.D Gill — 1955
Capt. B. Ludwig — 1957
Capt. J. Collins — 1957-

The VICTORIA CROSS was awarded posthumously to Capt. A. Bisset Smith, Royal Naval Reserve in 1917.

During the 1939-45 war 176 Gordonians gave their lives in the Services.

The contingent at present consists of a basic & an army section Its strength of seventy-one cadets is now smaller than in the immediate post-war years but it retains its health & vigour. The Contingent Pipe Band is held to be of a high standard Many ex-cadets enter the Officers Training Corps at University & others gain Commissions in The Territorial Army.

Above: Pages prepared by R.G.C. C.C.F. for inclusion in the record of the cadet movement in its centenary year presented to Her Majesty The Queen, 22nd July 1960

Senior cadets 1962-63:
Front Row: Colin Lamont, Bill Fraser, Peter Watson, Tom Mackie, Donald Galbraith, Stan Calder
Rear Row: Sandy Fowler, Malcolm Mowatt, Peter L.F. Hendry, John Lucan, Sandy Mitchell, Gordon Peterkin Riddler, Dougall Bennett

Major John G. Dow M.B.E

Captain Tom Collins with Major John Dow
and Captain Bruce Simms

Glen Dye, 1986, with Captain Tom Collins, Major John Dow and Captain Bruce Simms

Glen Dye, 1986, with Bruce Simms, John Dow, Kevin Cowie & Andrew Hopps

Nijmegen Marches participants 1987: Ronnie Coutts, Cameron Humphries, Stuart Nicol, James Birt, Alan Douglas, Major John Dow, Andrew Mahaffy, Kevin Harvey, George Shearer, Henry Duncan, Alan Pepper, John Vermeulen *Photograph: Aberdeen Journals Ltd.*

H.R.H. The Duke of Edinburgh with cadets Joseph Baie, Hew Torrance, Rory McCLarty and Andrew Campbell at Cultybraggan July 1997. Brigadier Charles Grant (later Chief Executive of the Highland Reserve Forces and Cadets Association) is 3rd from the left

Colour Sgt. Emma Anderson, National Army Cadet Camp, British Columbia, 1994

Left: Andrew Hopps and cadets, Chalmain Gap, Cairngorms on C.C.F. Project circa 1996
Left hand group: Emma MacKay, Andrew Grant, Emma Anderson, Esther Krukowski, Capt. Andrew Hopps,
Standing centre: Derek Robertson
Right hand group: Gordon Campbell, Chris Brandon, Roddy Parker, Sean MacFarlane, Steven Jenkins (seated), Nils Reid, Gregor Mitchell, Dickon Brandon, (unidentified)

Senior cadets and staff, Cultybraggan 1993.
Front row: Lt. Margaret Ramsey, Capt. Kevin Cowie, R.S.M. James Pocock, Maj. Bruce Simms, Capt. Andrew Hopps, Lt. David Strang
Rear row: Steven Douglas (A), Grant Erskine (E), Neil Gair (TEK), Philip Whyte (A), Andrew Goodacre (C), Neil Ballantyne (TEK), Murray MacNaughtan (W)
At the time the Army Section was made up of 5 Platoons/Sections: Anzio, Corunna, El-Alamein, Tel-El Kebir, Waterloo. Letters in brackets indicate platoons.

Abseiling. Helena Rodnight at Loch Lednock Dam circa 1998

Captain Andrew Hopps

Lt. Andrew Hopps with cadet Greg Wilkie circa 1990

Capt. Kevin Cowie with H.R.H. the Duke of Edinburgh July 1997 at Cultybraggan

Capt. Kevin Cowie with C.C.F. group walking to Devil's Point, Cairngorms

ROBERT GORDON'S COLLEGE CCF

SCOTTISH CCF CENTRAL CAMP – CULTYBRAGGAN 1999

CAMP NOMINAL ROLL

Standing: Luke Bedford, Neil Malcolm, Alexander Compton, Philip Hare, Lauren Neal, Roseanne McCrae, Roy Fairhead, Nicholas Baker, Charles Howard, Andrew Bell, Chris Hendron (hidden), Andrew Johnston, Stephen Brown, Craig Brechin, Jamie Watt, Stuart Robertson (Best Cadet), Craig Thompson, Daniel Tope, David Mackie, Ross Mawdsley, Daniel Tope, Patrick Mockridge, Edward Gunn, Richard Tolstyko.

Kneeling: Kirsty Beaton (Best Recruit), Heather Cowie, Claire Kidd (Cadet Marksman), Ross Watt, Lucy Rennie, Alysha Whyte, Wayne Davies.

Seated: David Callan, Neil Cargill (CSM), Jonathan Coutts.

In Absentia: Tim Mackley, Andrew Krebs, Andrew Johnston.

Officers: Captain Kevin Cowie, Lt. Michael Maitland, Lt. David Morris.

Summer Camp Cultybraggan1999

And, if you bind us down
To paths which you ordain,
If you slay us in battles
Which you have caused
Then ask us to fight
How may you then
Expect us
To build a world fit for man
As a son of God?

The Henry Bittiner Prize for Poetry is awarded annually.

Flying Officer Iain R. Macaulay (R.G.C. 1938–41) was stationed at R.A.F. Dyce and died when the Mosquito reconnaissance aircraft in which he was training disappeared on a flight from Aberdeen to Stranraer. **Captain Alexander Hunter** (R.G.C. 1922–27) escaped from Sumatra ahead of the advancing Japanese Army. He lost his life during "a secret mission", later known to be a landing back on occupied Sumatra. **Rifleman William H. Jupp** (R.G.C. 1930–36) was killed in the Middle East and is buried in the El Alamein Cemetery. At the time his sister was serving as an officer in the W.R.N.S. at Portsmouth. **Lt Alastair Macdonald** (R.G.C. 1925–35) was presumed to have died on Sumatra, having been missing since the fall of Singapore. He was the son of Mr William N. Macdonald, a former member of the teaching staff of the College. **Charles S. M. Thom**, Hong Kong Volunteer Defence Corps, was killed in action on Christmas Day 1941, at the time of the surrender of Hong Kong. His family lived at 19 Powis Terrace and he had been a keen member of the St Andrew's Cathedral Company of the Boy Scouts.

One touching account is given concerning **Sgt Norman Fyfe**, 16 Mile-end Avenue, who was officially reported to have died during the evacuation of Singapore on 15th February 1942. He had been a talented junior footballer who was capped for Scotland against Wales in 1926:

> Near midnight on 15th February three of us made an escape attempt. Norrie led us to the Singapore Yacht Club, where we searched for some kind of sea-worthy boat for over an hour. We found a two-seater outrigger racing skiff in the hands of an Army officer. As the boat could hold no more than two, we tossed for the odd man out, and Norrie lost. We shook hands on the quay, and pushed off. (*Gordonian*, December 1946)

Charles Farquharson died in Changi Prisoner of War Camp, Singapore. He had been an engineer in Malaya and member of the Johore Volunteer Engineers. At the time of his death, his son, who lived at 13 Holburn St, was a pupil at the College.

Warrant Officer John F. Kelman (R.G.C. 1935–40) was amongst the first R.A.F. aircrew to train in the USA. He flew with his Spitfire squadron against the Japanese in the defence of Port Darwin and was credited with the destruction of two Japanese aircraft. He had played rugby for Gordonians and the North of Scotland.

Lt Philip Capes, Royal Engineers (R.G.C. 1935–38) was killed on 21st November 1944. He had been an apprentice architect with Messrs Tawse & Allan and a chorister at St John's Episcopal Church. His captain wrote:

> You would not know at the time when the B.B.C. mentioned in the news that the airfield at Reggio, the first in Italy, was already in use two days after the Allies had landed, that it was the good work of Philip and his men whom made it possible . . . His last words were "How are the others? Are

the others all right?" Those words best typify him: his foremost thoughts were always of others, and in particular the men of the platoon he commanded, in which there existed a mutual trust and affection the equal of which I have never previously known.

(*Gordonian*, June 1945, p. 3)

Decorations and Awards

Many Gordonians are mentioned as having been decorated for service, including several in the magazine of December 1941. A full list of Gordonians known to have been decorated follows in the Appendices to Part one.

Acting Wing Commander Ronald B. Thomson D.S.O., D.F.C, captained an aircraft which sank a U-Boat, an action after which he survived three and a half days in a dinghy. He had performed three successful attacks on U-Boats in six weeks. He had been Assistant Sports Master on the R.G.C. staff before representing the South of Scotland against the All-Blacks and Scotland against The Rest in 1935.

Senior Chaplain Rev. Alan J. Fraser (R.G.C. 1920–25) was Mentioned in Dispatches for services in the 1944 Burma campaign. He had been evacuated from France through Dunkirk in 1940. **Rev. Joseph Grant** M.C. served in North Africa, Italy and Greece. He was the son of a former Provost of Ballater and was minister of Rhynie before the war.

Lt Col. Ian Mackenzie received the D.S.O. from Field Marshal Montgomery. His parents lived in Johannesburg and his uncle, William A. Mackenzie, had delivered the Founder's Day Oration in 1942. **Major W. J. K Stark** O.B.E (R.G.C. 1903–06) was Malayan Government Representative in India. **Sub Lt William**

Still (R.G.C. 1936–41) was Mentioned in Dispatches for service in R.N. Commando landings in Normandy. **Captain Harry S. Cable** (1929–33) was awarded the Military Medal as a corporal at El Alamein and later the Military Cross. His brother, **Signalman Alexander Cable**, Royal Corps of Signals, (R.G.C. 1926–31) died of wounds on 10th March 1945.

Major-General Neil Cantlie, M.B., Ch. B. (R.G.C. 1905–09) was made a C.B. in the King's Birthday Honours in June 1947. He was Honorary Physician to H.M. The King and Director-General of Army Medical Services.

Col. George R. McRobert (R.G.C. 1905–12) was knighted in the King's Birthday Awards 1947. He graduated in Medicine from the University of Aberdeen and served in the Royal Army Medical Corps in the First World War. He entered the Indian Medical Service in 1920 and became Professor of Medicine at Rangoon University in 1925. In 1945 he was appointed Inspector-General of Civil Hospitals, Bihar, India.

Col. David Levack T.D., President of the Gordonian Association, was invested with the C.B.E. by H.M. The King at a ceremony at Buckingham Palace on 10th June 1947 in recognition of "gallantry and distinguished services in the field".

Once again, only a few examples of war service given by Gordonians appear here and it is quite impossible to give a full account of the contribution made by our former pupils. What is clear is that during the war years the Governors and College staff were quick to respond to the need to provide opportunities for boys to prepare themselves for military involvement as they progressed through their education. Those returning home at the end of the war would, for the second time in only a few years, find a Gordonian community coming to terms with tremendous loss.

Chapter Seven

THE END OF HOSTILITIES

Following the end of the Second World War the future of cadet organizations was very uncertain with, once again, a backlash against military training for its own sake. As L. J. Collins states in *Cadets and the War*:

> The A.C.F. was wary of what happened at the end of the First World War when the Territorial Cadet Force of the time was wholly committed to military training. In 1918 people generally were so devastated by the enormity of the first universal conflict and the horrendous casualty list, that their interest in military service decreased sharply ... (p.116)

If the cadet movement were to be seen as viable, desirable and relevant in post-war society, a return to the other main philosophy behind training would be required:

> As a result of the change in emphasis, with the cadets' military training being geared to the development of the individual as a member of society rather than just the production of a future soldier, sailor or airman, the phrase "citizenship training" became a cornerstone of all cadet training. (p.117)

The B.N.C.A. changed its name to the Army Cadet Force Association and this name is still in use today. With the end of training as a means of preparing cadets for immediate war service, a change of direction was welcomed. Going back to the ideas of Octavia Hill, it was recognised that the Cadet Forces provided the ideal opportunity to develop personality, leadership skills and a sense of citizenship. Adventurous Training and later the Duke of Edinburgh's Award Scheme were introduced. It was also recognised that, with the end of hostilities and National Service, the supply of potential cadet officers from former regular servicemen would gradually dry up. Over a period of time, officers would come to be recruited from former members of the Cadet Forces themselves.

R.G.C. Army Cadet Force remained active throughout the period 1945–48 with several enjoyable camps at, for example, Braemar. Other activities remained popular.

Although the College A.T.C. unit ceased to operate, College boys remained active in cadet units outside the school. Class VC pupil Flt Sgt Norman Wilson of No.107 Sqn. A.T.C. was selected, along with nineteen cadets from various parts of the UK, to visit the British Zone in Germany in April 1947.

After being given the "customary once over from the M.O." and exchanging money into B.A.F. tokens they flew from Hendon in Anson and Dominie aircraft and passed over Dunkirk before arriving at their destination of Bückeburg.

They visited the viaduct at Bielefeld, destroyed by Grand Slam bombs of 617 (Dambusters) Sqn. on 14th March 1945 and the Möhne Dam, one of the targets of the original Dambusters raid on 16th May 1943. Norman wrote:

> The dam has been completely rebuilt, but of the accompanying power-station nothing remains but a mass of twisted pipes and girders. (*Gordonian*, June 1947, p.194)

The Germans to whom they spoke, he wrote, "did not seem to be too badly off and appeared resigned to their circumstances". He does however note that:

> "it was painful to see the Germans have to pay as much as 7 Marks (3/6) for one cigarette, whereas people here complain

about paying twopence each for them ... Wherever we went there were stretches of desolation and squalor for the homes of the German town-dwellers are at present far below the standard of those of a normal civilised community. (p. 194)

Thoughts turned once again to the idea of a memorial to Gordonians who had died in the recent war. The Editorial in the June 1946 *Gordonian* looked to the future:

All of us have had to face the loss in war of those dear to us; but we who are members of the Gordonian family have before us, too, that pitifully long roll of honour bearing the names of those whom we knew, and whose death we know only too well has robbed the world of such men as can ill be spared. Now the time has come to take new resolution that we may face the problems which weigh upon us, and work that their lives have not been given in vain.

The problem of a war memorial is a difficult one; but in our time the general view is that honour may best be paid to the fallen by ensuring that the spirit of communal effort and sacrifice should be perpetuated. (p. 82)

There was lengthy debate and a great deal of support for something that would "encourage the companionship which school-days made valuable and, in the upshot, foster the traditions of our school, traditions which modern trends in education seem to endanger" (*Gordonian*, December 1946, p. 122) and which would be "more than stone and mortar" (*Gordonian*, December 1947, p. 220). It was proposed that a room, or rooms, within the College might be given over to the Gordonian Association to provide permanent accommodation for members of the Association. This project was many years in coming, but the eventual outcome was the Seafield Club, situated only a matter of yards from the sports field, the Association's First World War memorial. The idea of a memorial chapel was put forward but eventually rejected. The Association did however install a modern Compton electronic church organ in the MacRobert Hall as a memorial which would play a major part in the life of the whole school. The organ was dedicated on 15th October 1951 by the Rev. T. B. Stewart M.C., T.D., D.D., Chaplain to His Majesty The King. Many Gordonians will remember morning assembly when hymn singing was accompanied by the organ with its memorial plaque clearly visible from the front rows of the MacRobert Hall.

APPENDICES

PART ONE

ROLL OF HONOUR:
THE FIRST WORLD WAR

Alexander T Adam
Pioneer
Royal Engineers
2 December 1917
Faubourg Diamiens Cemetery,
Arras
Grave/Memorial Reference: VI A 30

James H Adams
Pte
Cameron Highlanders
25 September 1915

John T M Alexander
Pte
Gordon Highlanders
27 May 1915
Cabaret-Rouge British Cemetery,
Souchez
XVII E 11

John Allan, M.C.
Capt.
Machine Gun Corps
9 June 1917
Bailleul Communal Cemetery
III C 100

Alexander Allardyce
Sgt
Gordon Highlanders
25 September 1915
Ypres (Menin Gate) Memorial

Alexander K Anderson
Spr
R.E.
14 February 1919
Mons (Bergen) Communal
Cemetery
X B 43

Alexander S Anderson
Sgt
R.E.
14 August 1917

David Anderson
Pte
Gordon Highlanders
23 April 1917
Roeux British Cemetery
B 14

Henry A Anderson
2/Lt
Gordon Highlanders
21 July 1918
Terlincthun British Cemetery,
Wimille
XVI AA 18

Hugh C Anderson
Capt.
Canadian Expeditionary Force
11 August 1917
Poperinghe New Military
Cemetery
II H 20

William B Anderson, M.C.
2/Lt
Gordon Highlanders
7 April 1917
Maroeuil British Cemetery
IV D 7

Norman J Angus
2/Lt
Gordon Highlanders
18 September 1917
Etaples Military Cemetery
XXIII A 10

William Angus
Lt Col
R.A.M.C.
23 August 1919
Nellfield Cemetery, Aberdeen
Grave I.1321

Malcolm R Bain
L. Cpl
Seaforth Highlanders
6 August 1916
Thiepval Memorial
Pier & Face 15 C

James K Barnet
Lt
Royal Scots & R.A.S.C. (MT)
2 November 1918
Cairo War Memorial
Q 58

Alexander W Baxter
Pte
Seaforth Highlanders &
Northumberland F
12 May 1918
Berlin South-Western Cemetery
VI E 6

John A Begg
Pioneer
R.E.
31 August 1917
Bucquoy Road Cemetery, Ficheux
I L 4

John H Begg
Capt.
Gordon Highlanders
4 August 1916

Clifford T Bell
Capt.
R.A.M.C.
2 February 1919
Allenvale Cemetery, Aberdeen
Grave C104

John Benson
Sgt
R.F.C.
23 June 1916
Dar es Salaam War Cemetery
5 G 3

Bernard G Beveridge, M.C.
Capt.
R.A.M.C.
21 March 1918
Bancourt British Cemetery
I F 12

Joseph P Beveridge
Capt.
Gordon Highlanders
20 October 1918

George Beverley
Pte
Gordon Highlanders
15 November 1916
Mailly Wood Cemetery, Mailly-
Maillet
I B 23

William J G Birnie
Lt
Gordon Highlanders & Royal Tank
Corps
23 November 1917
Cambrai Memorial, Louverval
Panel 10

Norman Birss
Sgt
Gordon Highlanders
13 November 1916
Thiepval Memorial
Pier & Face 15B & 15C

David P Bisset
Pte
Australian Imperial Force
19 September 1918
Le Cateau Military Cemetery
I B 115

John Black
Capt.
Kings Own Royal Regiment
26 September 1917
St Sever Cemetery, Rouen
Officers B I 25

Charles F Blake
L. Cpl
Royal Scots
10 October 1918
Angreau Community Cemetery
I D 13

James Booth, M.C.
Lt
Machine Gun Corps
6 November 1918
Angreau Community Cemetery
I A 12

Victor A Booth
Drv.
R.F.A.
17 February 1915
Bethune Town Cemetery
IV A 22

William J G Booth
Pte
R.A.M.C.
28 September 1918
Sarigol Militery Cemetery, Kriston
D 693

Adam N Bothwell
Pte
Gordon Highlanders
13 November 1916
Mailly Wood Cemetery, Mailly-
Maillet
I F 5

John Bowie
Cpl
R.E.
27 June 1916
Heilly Station Cemetery, Mericourt
- L'Abbe
I F 6

John B Boyd
Lt
Gordon Highlanders
21 March 1918
Arras Memorial
Bay 8 & 9

Robert M Boyd
Capt.
R.A.M.C.
13 December 1918

H Brian Brooke
Capt.
Gordon Highlanders
24 July 1916
Springbank Cemetery, Aberdeen
N 19

George A Brown
Pte
Gordon Highlanders
6 July 1916
Louez Mil Cem Duisans
I D 7

Thomas B Brown
Gnr
R.F.A.
28 May 1917
Bedford House Cemetery
Enc 4 I I 62

William Bruce, M.C.
2/Lt
R.E.
3 December 1918
Soumoy Commual Cemetery
I

George M Calder
2/Lt
Seaforth Highlanders
25 September 1915
Dud Corner Cemetery, Loos
V H 1

George Callum
Pte
Gordon Highlanders
23 April 1915
Arras Memorial
Bay 8 & 9

Archibald J. F. Campbell
Pte
Gordon Highlanders
21 September 1917
Dozinghem Military Cemetery
VII C 11

Alexander C Chapman
Pte
Gordon Highlanders
25 September 1915
Ypres (Menin Gate) Memorial
Pan 38

R Erskine Christie
L. Cpl
South African Scottish Rifles
11 April 1918
Ypres (Menin Gate) Memorial
Pan 15-16 16A

William Chrystall
Pte
Black Watch
10 April 1918
Loos Memorial
Pan 78-83

James M Clark
Spr
R.E.
1 October 1916

Douglas B Cochran
Pte
Gordon Highlanders
9 April 1917

James K Collie
Pte
Gordon Highlanders
16 December 1916
Allenvale Cemetery, Aberdeen

Ferguson Connon
Cpl
Cameronians (Scottish Rifles)
25 April 1918
Tyne Cot Memorial
Pan 68-70/162

Francis A Corbett
Bdr
R.F.A.
2 April 1917
Maroeuil British Cemetery
IV B 6

John M Coutts
Pte
Australian Imperial Force (Inf)
11 October 1917
Ypres (Menin Gate) Memorial
Pan 7-17-23-25-27-29

William Coutts
Pte
London Scottish
17 July 1916
Thiepval Memorial
Pier & Face 9C & 13C

Alexander Cruden
Pte
Gordon Highlanders
23 May 1917
Arras Memorial
Bay 8 & 9

Alexander T Cruickshank
Spr
R.E.
14 February 1919
Mons (Bergen) Communal
Cemetery
X B 5

Harold A Cruickshank
Lt
Royal Scots Fusiliers
28 September 1915
Bethune Town Cemetery
II K 1

William S Cruickshank
Pte
Gordon Highlanders
27 May 1915

Marianus R Cumming
L. Cpl
Gordon Highlanders
13 June 1915
Ypres (Menin Gate) Memorial
Pan 38

Alfred J Davidson
Pte
Gordon Highlanders
5 August 1916
Dantzig Alley British Cemetery,
Mametz
I A 45

Peter F Davidson
Pte
Black Watch
16 May 1917
Athies Communal Cemetery
K 13

William A Davidson
2/Lt
Gordon Highlanders
2 July 1916
Morlancourt British Cemetery
A 30

Henry G Davie
Pte
Australian Imperial Forces
20 May 1917
Grevillers British Cemetery
V E 12

James Dawson
2/Lt
Durham Light Infantry
28 May 1918

George Dewar
Lt
R.A.M.C.
3 February 1916
Humber Camps Communal
Cemetery
II A 2

William Diack
2/Lt
Gordon Highlanders
20 September 1917
Tyne Cot Memorial
Pan 135-136

Robert Donald
Sgt
Gordon Highlanders
9 June 1916
Louez Military Cemetery, Duisans
I D 5

William Donald
Pte
Gordon Highlanders
25 September 1915
Ypres (Menin Gate) Memorial
Pan 138

William S D Donaldson
Pte
R.A.M.C.
28 July 1916
Dartmoor Cemetery, Becordel-
Becourt
I E 63

William Dougall, M.C.
Lt
Canadian Expeditionary Force
21 July 1918
Jonchery-sur-Vesle British Cemetery
I H 28

William Duffus
Pte
Gordon Highlanders
1 December 1917
Rocquigny-Equancourt Road
British Cemetery, Manancourt
V B 19

James Duguid
2/Lt
North Staffordshire Regiment
9 April 1916
Basra Memorial
Pan 34

Alexander D Duncan
L. Sgt
Gordon Highlanders
25 June 1915
Wimereux Commual Cemetery
I J 4

Henry C Duncan
Gnr
R.F.A.
22 October 1915
Worms (Hochheim Hill) Cemetery
Screen Wall

Andrew F Edward
Gnr
R.F.A.
18 April 1918
Fouquieres Churchyard
II F 2

Ernest G Elmslie
2/Lt
Royal Scots
26 September 1917
Tyne Cot Memorial
Pan 11-14 & 162

Edgar H. Ewen
Lt
Royal Scots Fusiliers
1 May 1917
Troon Cemetery, Ayrshire
B Old 178

John B Ewen
Pte
Gordon Highlanders
25 September 1915
Ypres (Menin Gate) Memorial
Pan 38

John M Falconer
Pte
Highland Light Infantry
1 July 1916
Thiepval Memorial
Pier & Face 15C

Robert Falconer
C.S.M.
Gordon Highlanders
23 July 1916
Caterpillar Valley Cemetery,
Longueval
XII E 27

George Farquhar
Pte
Gordon Highlanders
14 November 1916
Mailly Wood Cemetery, Mailly-
Maillet
I L 12

James Farquhar
Capt.
R.A.M.C.
January 1920
Allenvale Cemetery, Aberdeen
D35

Ian Farquharson
2/Lt
Gordon Highlanders
22 August 1918
St Hilaire Cemetery, Frevent
M 28

Joseph D Farquharson
Cpl
Gordon Highlanders
20 September 1917
Tyne Cot Memorial
Pan 135-136

William B Farquharson
Pte
Royal Fusiliers
11 April 1917
Faubourg D'Amiens Cemetery,
Arras
VII G 16

William B Ferguson
Pte
Seaforth Highlanders
20 July 1918
Gonnehem British Cemetery
F 7

James Findlay
2/Lt
Northumberland Fusiliers
16 June 1917
Arras Memorial
Bay 2 & 3

Henry G Fraser
Pte
R.A.M.C.
20 August 1916
Caterpillar Valley Cemetery,
Longueval
X E 14

Ian C Fraser
2/Lt
Argyll & Sutherland Highlanders
25 September 1915
Cambrin Church Yard
B 8

Ronald H B Fraser
Pte
Royal Fusiliers
25 March 1918
Arras Memorial
Bay 3

George Fyfe
Pte
Gordon Highlanders
2 April 1915
Ypres (Menin Gate) Memorial
Pan 38

Leslie Fyfe
Pte
Gordon Highlanders
23 July 1916
Thiepval Memorial
Pier & Face 15B & C

Robert J Fyfe
Lt
R.F.C.
18 June 1917

John Galloway
Cpl
Australian Imp Forces (Tasmania)
17 January 1917
Springbank Cemetery, Aberdeen
Grave N.89

James R G Garbutt
Lt
R.A.M.C.
1 December 1915
Vermelles British Cemetery
I F 5

Willijohn O Gilmour
2/Lt
Scottish Horse
15 May 1917
Doiran Memorial

Robert Glegg
2/Lt
R.E.
19 July 1915
Cabaret-Rouge British Cemetery,
Souchez
XVII C 26

Charles Gordon
Lt
Canadian Expeditionary Force
5 October 1916
Vimy Memorial

George G Gordon
Cpl
Gordon Highlanders
14 June 1915
Bedford House Cemetery
Enc. No. 2 V B 35

James T Gordon
Engineer
Mercantile Marine
20 August 1917
Tower Hill Memorial

Alexander Grant
Capt.
Gordon Highlanders
13 November 1916
Mailly Wood Cemetery, Mailly-
Maillet
I A 23

John S Grant, M.C.
Capt. The Rev.
Gordon Highlanders
9 April 1917
Highland Cemetery, Roclincourt
I A 47

David A Gray
Cpl
R.E.
24 May 1917
Level Cross Cemetery, Fampoux

George H Gray
2/Lt
R.A.M.C.
28 April 1916

Herbert S Gray
Cpl
19 September 1917
Bleuet Farm Cemetery
I D 4

Alexander Guthrie
Lt
R.F.A.
12 July 1917
Ramscappelle Road Military
Cemetery
Nieuport Mil. Cem. Mem. 1

William S Haig
Cpl
Gordon Highlanders
25 September 1915
Ypres (Menin Gate) Memorial
Pan 38

John M Hall
2/Lt
Northumberland Fusiliers
1 July 1916
Thiepval Memorial
Pier & Face 10B 11B

Andrew P Hay
2/Lt
Kings Own Scottish Borderers
30 April 1916
Auchonvillers Military Cemetery
II D 18

Edward H Hay
2/Lt
Gordon Highlanders
11 June 1917
Duisans British Cemetery, Etrun
IV J 17

William L Hay
Pte
R.A.M.C.
3 July 1918

Alexander R Henderson
Lt
Gordon Highlanders
25 September 1915
Ypres (Menin Gate) Memorial
Pan 38

George A F Henderson
Lt
R.F.C.
4 July 1918
Longside New Churchyard
Grave 508

James M Henderson, M.C.
Maj.
Gordon Highlanders
11 April 1918
Loss Memorial
Pan 115-119

Gordon Hendry
L. Cpl
Gordon Highlanders
25 August 1918
Vis-en-Artois Memorial
Pan 10

Douglas J L Hendry
2/Lt
Gordon Highlanders
25 September 1917
Dozinghem Military Cemetery
V F 17

Robert F D High
Lt
Gordon Highlanders
22 March 1918
Arras Memorial
Bay 8 & 9

Alexander R Horne
L. Cpl
Gordon Highlanders
25 January 1917
Allenvale Cemetery, Aberdeen
Grave C69

Joseph L Horne
Bdr
R.F.A.
9 April 1919
Allenvale Cemetery, Aberdeen
Grave L84

Adam G Howitt, M.C.
Capt.
East Surrey Regiment
5 August 1917
Ypres (Menin Gate) Memorial
Pan 34

William Hunter
Pte
Royal Fusiliers
28 October 1918
Allenvale Cemetery, Aberdeen
Grave D1880

Alexander Hustwick
L. Cpl
Gordon Highlanders
13 June 1915
Ypres (Menin Gate) Memorial
Pan 38

John W Ingram
Pte
Canadian Expeditionary Force
24 April 1915
Ypres (Menin Gate) Memorial
Pan 18-24-26-30

James J Innes
Pte
London Scottish
3 January 1915
Le Touret Memorial
Pan 45

James D Ironside
Spr
R.E.
12 March 1917
St Peter's Cemetery, Aberdeen
Grave WD18.43

Donald F Jenkins, M.C.
2/Lt
Seaforth Highlanders
13 November 1916
Mailly Wood Cemetery, Mailly-
Maillet
I B 27

John Johnston
2/Lt
R.E.
10 April 1918
Tyne Cot Memorial
Pan 8 & 162

Robert Jolly
2/Lt
Gordon Highlanders
26 November 1919
St Cyrus Upper (Parish)
Churchyard
Grave 2.4

Alexander W Joss
Pte
Highland Light Infantry
16 July 1916
Thiepval Memorial
Pier & Face 15C

Terence O'N W Kelly
2/Lt
Gordon Highlanders
2 May 1917
Etaples Military Cemetery
XVII C 13

Charles Kemp
Lt
Royal Scots
25 May 1915
Helles Memorial
Pan 26-30

Robert Kennedy
Pte
Gordon Highlanders
24 April 1915
Wytschaete Military Cemetery
II F 5

Francis Kerrin
Pte
Highland Light Infantry
18 November 1916
Frankfurt Trench British Cemetery,
Beaumont-Hamel
C 28

Arthur G Kirkland
Spr
R.E.
21 March 1918
Arras Memorial
Bay 7

Walter A Knight
Pte
Black Watch
24 June 1918
Cologne Southern Cemetery
XII G 24

Harry D Laing
Capt.
Gordon Highlanders
13 March 1915
Le Touret Memorial
Pan 39-41

Thomas Laing
I A 21

Alexander Larg
Pte
Artists' Rifles
13 May 1918
New Southgate Cemetery
L 930

Thomas B Law
Surgeon
R.N. Troopships
15 November 1918

James W Leith
L. Sgt
Queens Own Cameron
Highlanders
14 October 1919
Thiepval Memorial
Pier & Face 15B

George A Leslie
L. Cpl
Gordon Highlanders
30 July 1917
Dozinghem Military Cemetery
II A 14

William Leslie
Capt.
R.G.A.
12 January 1916
Maala Cemetery
Sp. Plot 1.7

David Livingstone
Lt
R.N.R.
15 February 1918
Portsmouth Naval Memorial
30

George Low
2/Lt
Gordon Highlanders
25 September 1915
Ypres (Menin Gate) Memorial
Pan 38

John Low
2/Lt
King's Royal Rifle Corps
10 January 1918
Tyne Cot Memorial
Pan 115-9, 162 & 163A

James Lunan
Lt
Gordon Highlanders
20 September 1917
Poelcapelle British Cemetery
XL V E 12

Harry Lyon
Pte
Gordon Highlanders
16 June 1915
Ypres (Menin Gate) Memorial
Pan 38

John A McCombie
Sgt
Gordon Highlanders
25 July 1916
Heilly Station Cemetery,
Mericourt-L'Abbe
II C 60

Donald J R McConnochie
Sgmn
R.F.A.
7 August 1916
Dantzig Alley British Cemetery,
Mametz
IX S 2

Charles MacGregor
CQS
Gordon Highlanders
14 May 1916
Calais Southern Cemetery
C 4 10

Duncan McGregor
L. Cpl
Gordon Highlanders
25 September 1915
Ypres (Menin Gate) Memorial

John McHardy
Lt
Gordon Highlanders
24 July 1918
Buzancy Military Cemetery
III D 6

William Machray, D.C.M.
Sgt
Royal Scots
12 October 1917
Tyne Cot Memorial
XIV E 4

Keith MacKay
Cpl
Gordon Highlanders
28 April 1915
Bailleul Communal Cemetery
I B 23

Alexander McKenzie
Lt
R.A.M.C.
25 May 1919
St Peter's Cemetery, Aberdeen
Grave DWSD11.4

Leslie McKenzie
Lt
Black Watch
2 April 1918
Etaples Military Cemetery
XXVIII G 6

Arthur G Mackie
Lt
Canadian Expeditionary Force
9 April 1917
Vimy Memorial

John Mackie
Sgt
Australian Imperial Forces
28 April 1918
Meteren Military Cemetery
V F 734

Francis MacKinnon
Capt.
Gordon Highlanders
16 May 1915
Guards Cemetery, Windy Corner,
Cuinchy
III T 25

James McLaggan, M.C.
Capt.
R.A.M.C.
4 October 1918
Prospect Hill Cemetery, Gouy
II D 14

Ian M McLaren
Pte
Royal Fusiliers
7 October 1916

John S McMillan
Lt
Royal Scots Fusiliers (King's
African Rifles)
12 March 1918
Dar Es Salaam War Cemetery
4 C 4

William B McPherson
Midshipman
R.N.
23 October 1917

John E McQueen
Lt Col
Gordon Highlanders
25 September 1915
Loos Memorial
Pan 115-119

William McQuiban
Capt.
R.A.M.C.
2 May 1918
Kantara War Memorial Cemetery
E 266

A McLean Maitland
2/Lt
R.E.
1 August 1916
Norfolk Cemetery Becordel-
Becourt
I D 108

Alexander D Marr
Sgt
Gordon Highlanders
13 October 1915
Authuile Military Cemetery
B 48

Charles S Marr
Pte
Canadian Expeditionary Force
3 March 1916
Bordon Military Cemetery
Pres. B 5

William Martin
Appr.
Mercantile Marine, S.S. *Otaki*
10 March 1917
Tower Hill Memorial

John H S Mason
Pte
Gordon Highlanders
25 September 1915
Ypres (Menin Gate) Memorial
Pan 38

William Matthew
Spr.
R.E.
12 March 1917
Etaples Military Cemetery
XXII A 2

John A Matthews, M.M.
Cpl
Gordon Highlanders
23 May 1918
Cologne Southern Cemetery
VIII B 13

William Meff
2/Lt
R.F.C.
25 July 1918
Allenvale Cemetery, Aberdeen
Grave D.1597

William M S Merson
Capt.
Gordon Highlanders
13 November 1916
Mailly Wood Cemetery, Mailly-Maillet
I B 24

Robert H Middleton
Pte
Gordon Highlanders
1 June 1915
Ypres (Menin Gate) Memorial
Pan 38

Allan S Milne
2/Lt
Gordon Highlanders
26 June 1916
Poperinghe New Military Cemetery
II A 32

Frederick W Milne
Pte
Gordon Highlanders
2 October 1915
Ypres (Menin Gate) Memorial
Pan 38

James J S Milne
Pte
Gordon Highlanders
13 April 1918

John W H Milne
Pte
Royal Fusiliers
17 February 1917
Regina Trench Cemetery,
Grandcourt
IV D 18

George Minty
Capt.
Gordon Highlanders
23 November 1917
Orival Wood Cemetery, Flesquieres
I A 4

Alexander Mitchell
Pte
Gordon Highlanders
25 September 1915
Loos Memorial
Pan 115-119

Andrew Mitchell
Pte
Canadian Expeditionary Force
1915

George B Mitchell
Pte
Gordon Highlanders
13 September 1918
Leuze Communal Cemetery
II D 2

Peter H Mitchell, M.C.
2/Lt
Gordon Highlanders
14 September 1917
Mendinghem Military Cemetery
VII C 6

Robert T L Mitchell
Lt
Gordon Highlanders
29 November 1919

Charles P Moir
Pte
Royal Fusiliers
30 November 1917
Tincourt New British Cemetery
III B 1

Alfred G Morris
2/Lt
Gordon Highlanders
10 June 1916
Aubigny Communal Cemetery
V A 10

Andrew D Munro
Pte
Gordon Highlanders
19 May 1917
Arras Memorial
Bay 8 & 9

Herbert Murray, M.C.
Capt.
Gordon Highlanders
20 July 1918
Marfaux British Cemetery
I B 7

James S Murray
Spr
R.E.
27 May 1915
Cabaret-Rouge British Cemetery,
Souchez
XVII E 13

John G W Murray
Pte
Gordon Highlanders
25 September 1915
Ypres (Menin Gate) Memorial
Pan 38

Murdo M Murray
Pte
Queens Own Cameron
Highlanders
25 September 1915
Loos Memorial
Pan 119-124

Robert W S Murray
Capt.
R.A.M.C. & R.F.C.
6 May 1919
Cairo War Memorial Cemetery
P 21

J M Stewart Paterson
Pte
Gordon Highlanders
22 April 1915
Wytschaete Military Cemetery
Sp. Mem. B 5

John F Philip
Lt
R.N.R.
18 November 1917
Plymouth Naval Memorial
23

Stanley H Pilkington
2/Lt
R.F.C., Australian Air Force
24 October 1917
Brookwood Military Cemetery
XI D 20

L George Proctor
Tpr
Canadian Forces
31 May 1921
Toronto (Prospect) Cemetery
Vererans 1001

John Proctor
Major
R.A.M.C.
12 August 1918
Boves East Communal Cemetery
A 1

Lewis N G Ramsay
2/Lt
Gordon Highlanders
21 March 1915
Estaires Communal Cemetery
II H 6

Edwin J Reid
L. Cpl
Liverpool Scottish
11 August 1916
Corbie Communal Cemetery
2 A 88

Hugh Reid
2/Lt
Gordon Highlanders
23 July 1918
Marfaux British Cemetery
II H 4

John Reid
Sgt
Gordon Highlanders
13 March 1915
Le Touret Memorial
Pan 39-41

William M Reid
Pte
South African Scottish
3 January 1917
St Hilaire Cemetery, Frevent
I G 5

Alexander C Riddell
L. Cpl
Gordon Highlanders
25 September 1915
Loos Memorial
Pan 115-119

James Robertson
Lt Col
R.A.M.C.
21 March 1918
Bancourt British Cemetery
I F 11

Norman J Robertson
Cpl
Gordon Highlanders
30 May 1916
Aubigny Communal Cemetery
I C 47

William Robertson
Sgt
Royal Scots
19 November 1916
Etaples Military Cemetery
XX A 7

John Rose
Pte
Gordon Highlanders
30 May 1915
Ypres (Menin Gate) Memorial
Pan 38

Alistair Ross
2/Lt
R.F.C.
17 January 1916
Allenvale Cemetery, Aberdeen
Grave R49

David M Ross
Lt Cdr
R.N.R.
19 June 1919
Gore Hill Cemetery, Australia
Cong G 89 GRM2

George J Ross
2/Lt
Royal Scots Fusiliers
30 January 1918
Wanquetin Communal Cemetery
I C 15

William Ruddiman
Lt
Royal Scots
3 December 1916
Serre Road Cemetery No. 1
I D 20

Robert F Russell
Capt.
R.A.M.C.
22 April 1917
St Sever Cemetery, Rouen
Officers B 7 19

Thomas Ruxton
Pte
Gordon Highlanders
25 July 1919
Allenvale Cemetery, Aberdeen
Grave D. 140

Thomas H Sellar
Sgt
Gordon Highlanders (Machine
Gun Corps)
22 August 1918

John Shaw
2/Lt
Manchester Regiment
26 April 1918
Adelaide Cemetery, Villers-
Bretonneux
I B 4

Frank J Shepherd
Woolwich Arsenal
May 1917

Alexander Silver
Pte
Gordon Highlanders
25 September 1915
Ypres (Menin Gate) Memorial
Pan 38

John W Silver
2/Lt
Gordon Highlanders
26 October 1918
Auberchicourt British Cemetery
II F 2

Robert M Simpson
Pte
Black Watch
1 April 1917
Maroeuil British Cemetery
IV B 5

William W Singer
Tpr
Lothian & Border Horse
22 January 1916
Allenvale Cemetery, Aberdeen
Grave C. 975

Hugh H Skakle
Capt.
Gordon Highlanders
21 November 1917
Anneux British Cemetery
I E 2

Arthur Skene
Sgt
Gordon Highlanders
6 April 1917
Anzin - St Aubin British Cemetery
I A 17

Ian Skene, M.C.
2/Lt
Lancashire Fusiliers
12 April 1918
Valenciennes (St Roch) Communal
Cemetery
V D 28

Peter Skene
Pte
Seaforth Highlanders
25 October 1918
Harlebeke New British Cemetery
IV A 3

James A Slessor
Pte
Gordon Highlanders
18 February 1919
Brown's Copse Cemetery, Roeux
I B 5

Archibald Bissett Smith, V.C.
Lt
S.S. *Otaki* (Lt R.N.R.)
10 March 1917
Tower Hill Memorial

Charles T Smith
Lt
3rd Dragoon Guards
22 May 1915
Boulogne Eastern Cemetery
II B 48

Douglas R Smith
Capt.
R.E.
9 September 1918
St Pol British Cemetery, St Pol-sur-
Ternoise
II B 20

Francis J Smith, M.C.
2/Lt
Gordon Highlanders
16 May 1917
Brown's Copse Cemetery, Roeux
I C 39

James B Smith
2/Lt
Duke of Cornwall's L.I.
28 June 1918
Arras Memorial
Bay 6

Norman W Smith
L. Cpl
Australian Imp Forces
8 June 1917
Pont-D'Achelles Military Cemetery,
Nieppe
II A 13

Stephen Smith
Rfman
Queen Victoria Rifles
26 September 1917
Tyne Cot Memorial
Pan 151

William A Smith
Lt
R.A.M.C.
3 June 1917
Aubigny Communal Cemetery
VI G 16

Robert H Spittal
Capt.
R.A.M.C.
4 October 1917
Tyne Cot Memorial
Pan 160

David J S Stephen, M.C.
Capt.
R.A.M.C.
24 October 1917
Mendinghem Military Cemetery
VI B 3

John D Stephen
L. Cpl
Queen's Own Cameron
Highlanders
3 August 1917
Bleuet Farm Cemetery
I A 13

Robert Stephen
L. Cpl
Royal Fusiliers
1 July 1916
Hawthorn Ridge Cemetery No. 1
Auchonville
A 11

Alexander L Strachan
Surg. Prob.
R.N.V.R.
23 October 1916
Portsmouth Naval Memorial
24

Hector Strachan
Pte
Seaforth Highlanders
13 October 1918
Auberchicourt British Cemetery
II C 8

Francis L Stuart
Gnr
R.F.A.
3 May 1918
Couin British Cemetery
D 27

Joseph Summers
L. Cpl
Gordon Highlanders
20 June 1915
Wimereux Commual Cemetery
I J 3

Richard Surtees
Pte
Gordon Highlanders
13 December 1916
Doullens Communal Cemetery
III F 11

Robert Sutherland
Cpl
R.E.
22 March 1918
Arras Memorial
Bay 1

William H Sutherland, M.C.
2/Lt
Gordon Highlanders
23 March 1918
Arras Memorial
Bay 8 & 9

Bertram W Tawse
Sgt
Queen's Own Cameron
Highlanders
26 September 1916
Loos Memorial
Pan 119-124

Andrew J B Taylor
Pte
Gordon Highlanders
28 December 1916
Contay British Cemetery, Contay
VII B 8

Arthur Taylor
Pte
Gordon Highlanders
23 April 1917
Arras Memorial
Bay 8 & 9

John V S Taylor
Gnr
R.G.A.
9 April 1917
Sun Quarry Cemetery, Cherisy
G 15

Walter Taylor
2/Lt
Gordon Highlanders
30 July 1916
Thiepval Memorial
Pier & Face 15B & C

William F M Taylor
Sgt
Gordon Highlanders
21 March 1918
Arras Memorial
Bay 8 & 9

James M Teunon
2/Lt
R.G.A.
30 December 1918
Turriff Cemetery
Grave C. 549

John G Thom
L. Cpl
Gordon Highlanders
16 May 1917
Duisans British Cemetery, Etrun

Henry W Thomson
L. Cpl
Canadian Expeditionary Force
5 May 1917
Vimy Memorial

John A Thomson
Pte
Gordon Highlanders
28 April 1915

J Walter S Thomson
Lt
Gordon Highlanders
11 April 1918
Loos Memorial
Pan 115-119

Francis C Urquhart
Lt
Royal Scots
13 April 1918
Haringhe (Bandaghem) Military
Cemetery
II B 7

William Urquhart
Lt
Black Watch
7 August 1916
Thiepval Memorial

Walker
Pte
Canadian Expeditionary Force
16 August 1917

John E D Walker
R.E.
7 August 1917
II F 4

Robert S Walker
Sgmn
R.G.A.
4 November 1918
Reusnes Communal Cemetery
II C 3

William J Walker
R.S.M.
Gordon Highlanders
15 September 1917

Cecil A Warren
Pte
Seaforth Highlanders
3 July 1918
Allenvale Cemetery,
Aberdeen
Grave B. 77

William Watson
2/Lt
R.F.A.
19 January 1919
Allenvale Cemetery, Aberdeen
Grave K 330

David G M Watt
Pte
R.A.M.C.
26 April 1916
Strathdon Parish Churchyard
Near South Boundary

George B Watt
Pte
Seaforth Highlanders
9 May 1915
Le Touret Memorial
Pan 38 & 39

John B L B Watt
Pte
Gordon Highlanders
25 September 1915
Ypres (Menin Gate) Memorial
Pan 38

John S Watt
Pte
Gordon Highlanders
15 November 1916
Thiepval Memorial
Pier & Face 15B & C

William J Watt
Lt
Gordon Highlanders
25 September 1915
Dud Corner Cemetery, Loos
VIII F 9

Alexander Webster
Lt
R.F.C.
24 January 1919
Cologne Southern Cemetery
I D 11

Alexander Webster
2/Lt
Gordon Highlanders
9 April 1917
Roclincourt Military Cemetery
I A 5

George P Webster
Pte
Gordon Highlanders
11 May 1917
Arras Memorial
Bay 8 & 9

George Weir
Lt
R.H.A.
5 October 1918
St Germain-au-Mont-D'or
Communal Cemy.
B 4

John Williams
Pte
Gordon Highlanders
30 May 1915
Ypres (Menin Gate) Memorial

William C D Wilson
Capt
R.A.M.C.
18 September 1918
Godewaersvelde British
Cemetery
I P 15

RGC CASUALTIES OF
THE FIRST WORLD WAR:
GORDON HIGHLANDERS

Alexander	John T M	Pte		27 May 1915
Allardyce	Alexander	Sgt		25 September 1915
Anderson	David	Pte		23 April 1917
Anderson	Henry A	2/Lt		21 July 1918
Anderson	William B	2/Lt	M.C.	7 April 1917
Angus	Norman J	2/Lt		18 September 1917
Begg	John H	Capt.		4 August 1916
Beveridge	Joseph P	Capt.		20 October 1918
Beverley	George	Pte		15 November 1916
Birnie	William J G	Lt		23 November 1917
Birss	Norman	Sgt		13 November 1916
Bothwell	Adam N	Pte		13 November 1916
Boyd	John B	Lt		21 March 1918
Brooke	H Brian	Capt.		24 July 1916
Brown	George A	Pte		6 July 1916
Callum	George	Pte		23 April 1915
Campbell	Archibald J F	Pte		21 September 1917
Chapman	Alexander C	Pte		25 September 1915
Cochran	Douglas B	Pte		9 April 1917
Collie	James K	Pte		16 December 1916
Cruden	Alexander	Pte		23 May 1917
Cruickshank	William S	Pte		27 May 1915
Cumming	Marianus R	L. Cpl		13 June 1915
Davidson	Alfred J	Pte		5 August 1916
Davidson	William A	2/Lt		2 July 1916
Diack	William	2/Lt		20 September 1917
Donald	Robert	Sgt		9 June 1916
Donald	William	Pte		25 September 1915
Duffus	William	Pte		1 December 1917
Duncan	Alexander D	L. Sgt		25 June 1915
Ewen	John B	Pte		25 September 1915

Falconer	Robert	C.S.M.		23 July 1916
Farquhar	George	Pte		14 November 1916
Farquharson	Ian	2/Lt		22 August 1918
Farquharson	Joseph D	Cpl		20 September 1917
Fyfe	George	Pte		2 April 1915
Fyfe	Leslie	Pte		23 July 1916
Gordon	George G	Cpl		14 June 1915
Grant	Alexander	Capt.		13 November 1916
Grant	John S	Capt. The Rev.	M.C.	9 April 1917
Haig	William S	Cpl		25 September 1915
Hay	Edward H	2/Lt		11 June 1917
Henderson	Alexander R	Lt		25 September 1915
Henderson	James M	Maj.	M.C.	11 April 1918
Hendry	Gordon	L. Cpl		25 August 1918
Hendry	Douglas J L	2/Lt		25 September 1917
High	Robert F D	Lt		22 March 1918
Horne	Alexander R	L. Cpl		25 January 1917
Hustwick	Alexander	L. Cpl		13 June 1915
Jolly	Robert	2/Lt		26 November 1919
Kelly	Terence O'N W	2/Lt		2 May 1917
Kennedy	Robert	Pte		24 April 1915
Laing	Harry D	Capt.		13 March 1915
Leslie	George A	L/Cpl		30 July 1917
Low	George	2/Lt		25 September 1915
Lunan	James	Lt		20 September 1917
Lyon	Harry	Pte		16 June 1915
MacGregor	Charles	C.Q.S.		14 May 1916
MacKay	Keith	Cpl		28 April 1915
MacKinnon	Francis	Capt.		16 May 1915
Marr	Alexander D	Sgt		13 October 1915
Mason	John H S	Pte		25 September 1915
Matthews	John A	Cpl	M.M.	23 May 1918
McCombie	John A	Sgt		25 July 1916
McGregor	Duncan	L. Cpl		25 September 1915
McHardy	John	Lt		24 July 1918
McQueen	John E	Lt Col		25 September 1915
Merson	William M S	Capt.		13 November 1916
Middleton	Robert H	Pte		1 June 1915
Milne	Allan S	2/Lt		26 June 1916
Milne	Frederick W	Pte		2 October 1915
Milne	James J S	Pte		13 April 1918
Minty	George	Capt.		23 November 1917

Mitchell	Alexander	Pte		25 September 1915
Mitchell	George B	Pte		13 September 1918
Mitchell	Peter H	2/Lt	M.C.	14 September 1917
Mitchell	Robert T L	Lt		29 November 1919
Morris	Alfred G	2/Lt		10 June 1916
Munro	Andrew D	Pte		19 May 1917
Murray	Herbert	Capt.	M.C.	20 July 1918
Murray	John G W	Pte		25 September 1915
Paterson	J M Stewart	Pte		22 April 1915
Ramsay	Lewis N G	2/Lt		21 March 1915
Reid	Hugh	2/Lt		23 July 1918
Reid	John	Sgt		13 March 1915
Riddell	Alexander C	L. Cpl		25 September 1915
Robertson	Norman J	Cpl		30 May 1916
Rose	John	Pte		30 May 1915
Ruxton	Thomas	Pte		25 July 1919
Silver	Alexander	Pte		25 September 1915
Silver	John W	2/Lt		26 October 1918
Skakle	Hugh H	Capt.		21 November 1917
Skene	Arthur	Sgt		6 April 1917
Slessor	James A	Pte		18 February 1919
Smith	Francis J	2/Lt	M.C.	16 May 1917
Summers	Joseph	L. Cpl		20 June 1915
Surtees	Richard	Pte		13 December 1916
Sutherland	William H	2/Lt	M.C.	23 March 1918
Taylor	Andrew J B	Pte		28 December 1916
Taylor	Arthur	Pte		23 April 1917
Taylor	Walter	2/Lt		30 July 1916
Taylor	William F M	Sgt		21 March 1918
Thom	John G	L. Cpl		16 May 1917
Thomson	John A	Pte		28 April 1915
Thomson	J Walter S	Lt		11 April 1918
Walker	William J	R.S.M.		15 September 1917
Watt	John B L B	Pte		25 September 1915
Watt	John S	Pte		15 November 1916
Watt	William J	Lt		25 September 1915
Webster	Alexander	2/Lt		9 April 1917
Webster	George P	Pte		11 May 1917
Williams	John	Pte		30 May 1915

ROLL OF HONOUR:
THE SECOND WORLD WAR

Harry B Anderson
Ldg. Naval Airman
Fleet Air Arm
2 October 1941
Lee on Solent Memorial
Grave/Memorial Reference:
Bay 2, Panel 1

Alexander R Angus, O.B.E., M.C.
Warrant Bombardier (Surveyor)
R.A.
27 May 1940
Adegem Canadian War Cemetery
X1 H 12

Gavin A. E. Argo, M.C.
Lt Col
R.A.M.C.
15 March 1945
Durban (Stellawood) Cremation
Memorial

William A Barclay
Lt
R.E.
16 November 1944
Bergen-op-Zoom War Cemetery
1.A.3.

William B Barclay
Sgt Observer
R.A.F.
11 December 1942
Springbank Cemetery,
Aberdeen
Section T, Grave 190

John M Beaton
Ldg. Telegraphist
R.N.
18 September 1942
Chatham Naval Memorial
59, 2

George A Bisset
P.O.
R.A.F.V.R.
2 March 1943
Runnymede Memorial
Panel 123

Henry M Bittinger
Flt Sgt Navigator
R.A.F.
6 June 1944
Ranville War Cemetery
VIA.C. 1-25

Thomas D Breen
Sgt Observer
R.A.F.
11 December 1942
Allenvale Cemetery, Aberdeen
Section 2, Grave 66

Alan J W Brockie, M.C.
Capt.
R.A.
16 August 1944
Banneville-la-Campagne War
Cemetery
IV.A.11.

Alastair W Buchan
P.O.
R.A.F.
25/26 March 1942
Bergen General Cemetery
1 D 13

Joseph D Burnett
Capt.
R.A.S.C.
24 June 1943
Thanbyuzayat War Cemetery
B4 M 13

James H Burr
21 April 1943
City of Aberdeen Civilian Roll of
Honour

Kenneth R Butcher
Sgt Flight Eng.
R.A.F.
3/4 December 1943
Runnymede Memorial
Panel 114

Alexander Cable
Sig.
R.C. of Signals
10 March 1945
Taukkyan War Cemetery
20 D 1

Andrew Caie
Sgt
R.A.F.
31 May 1942
Allenvale Cemetery, Aberdeen
Section A, Grave 1005

Ashley Campbell
L.AC.
R.A.F.
10 August 1941
Springbank Cemetery, Aberdeen
Sec U, Grave 92A

Philip T Capes
Lt
R.E.
21 November 1944
Coriano Ridge War Cemetery
XV A 5

Gordon H M Carey
Flt Sgt
R.A.F.
28 June 1944
Aberlour Burial Ground
Grave 64

Edward F Chapman
Sgt Navigator
R.A.F.
8 June 1944
Harrogate (Stonefall) Cemetery
Sec. B Row E 19

Alexander W Cheyne
Flt Sgt
R.A.F.
29 Janaury 1943
Alamein Memorial
Col. 269

Harry W Cook
Flt Sgt
R.A.F.
21 July 1944
Runnymede Memorial
Panel 216

Douglas W S Cooper
Maj.
R.E. (Indian)
3 Februray 1944

William D Copland
Sgt
R.A.F.
1 December 1944
Springbank Cemetery, Aberdeen
Sec. U, Grave 70

Alexander V Cormack
F.O.
R.A.F.
20 March 1944
Runnymede Memorial
Panel 205

Sydney J Cormack
A.B.
Merchant Navy
7 December 1942
Tower Hill Memorial
Panel 25

Alexander B Cowie
Sgt
R.A.F.
8 March 1943
Allenvale Cemetery, Aberdeen
Sec. C, Grave 1959

Alexander D B Cowie
Sgt
R.E.
22 March 1943
Sfax War Cemetery
VII B 9

Ronald H Crabb
2/Lt
R.A.
7 June 1942
Feteresso Cemetery
Sec. L, Grave 64

David J W Cruickshank
P.O.
R.A.F.
21 November 1941
Halfaya Sollum War Cemetery
5 E 1-5

William A Cruickshank
P.O.
R.A.F.
19 October 1943
Malta (Capuccini) Naval Cemetery
Prot. Sec. (Men) Plot F 44

Douglas J Dalgarno
Maj.
Indian Army
October 1944
Delhi War Cemetery
2 K 11

George E Daniels
Flt Lt
R.C.A.F.
5 May 1942
Aberdeen Crematorium

Ronald Davidson
Sgt Air Gunner
R.A.F.
31 August 1944
Springbank Cemetery, Aberdeen
Sec. T, Grave 183

Harold S Davie
Sig.
R.C. of Signals
5 May 1940
Drumoak New Parish Cemetery
Grave 26

Laurence A Davie
Sgmn
R.C. of Signals
7 June 1940
Bayeux War Cemetery
X L 24

Alexander G Dawson
Sqn Ldr
R.A.F.
6 June 1944
Allenvale Cemetery, Aberdeen
Sec. 7, Grave 205A

Donald J Dawson
Flt Lt (Med)
R.A.F.
20 June 1944
Singapore Memorial
Col. 431

William Diack
Capt.
Gordon Highlanders
2 June 1940
London Cemetery, Longueval
13 F 39

John Dinnie
Radio Officer
Merchant Navy
28 March 1942
Tower Hill Memorial
Panel 105

John B Dougall
Second Officer
Merchant Navy
1942

James Douglas
Gunner
R.A.
23 May 1944
St Kentigern's R.C. Cemetery,
Glasgow
13 237

James G Duffus
Capt.
Gordon Highlanders
29 July 1943
Kirkee War Cemetery
3 AA 5

William Duguid
Lt
Queen's Own Cameron
Highlanders
25 February 1945
Mook War Cemetery
I A 15

James Duncan
Lt
Seaforth Highlanders
2 November 1942
El Alamein War Cemetery
XVII B 26

Malcolm C Duncan
Spr
R.E.
27 February 1943
Medjez-el-Bab Memorial
Face 10

Norman Duncan
2/Lt
Gordon Highlanders
14 May 1940
Allenvale Cemetery, Aberdeen
Sec. 2, Grave 81

Robert T Easton
Capt.
R.A.M.C.
1941
Suda Bay War Cemetery
3 E 5

Francis G Eddie
L. Cpl
York and Lancaster Regiment
25 December 1940
Springbank Cemetery, Aberdeen
Sec 9, Grave 176

David S Edmond
Sgt Gunner
R.A.F.
1941
Rheinberg War Cememtery
1 C 10

Alexander Ellis
F.O.
R.A.F.V.R.
d 29 October 1945
Springbank Cemetery, Aberdeen
Sec N, Grave 68A

Charles Farquharson
Capt.
Jahore Volunteer Engineers
June 1942

Ian D Forbes
Lt
Fife & Forfar Yeomanry R.A.C.
18 July 1944
Ranville War Cemetery
II D 10

Archibald N Forsyth
Surg. Cdr
R.N.
19 August 1941
Portsmouth Naval Memorial
Panel 45, Col. 3

Douglas P Fox, D.F.C. & Bar
Sqn Ldr
R.A.F.
12 June 1943
Uden War Cemetery
5 H 5-8

Albert V Frain
Eng. Officer
British India Steam and Navigation
Co
23 July 1945
Stanley Military Cemetery
4 A 17

James A Freeland
Seaman
R.N.
15 April 1944
Tullich Old Churchyard
Grave 114

Norman Fyfe
Sgt
F.M.S. Volunteer Force
15 February 1942
Singapore Memorial
Col. 392

Stanley M T Garrett
Spr
R.E.
3 March 1940
Escoublac-la-Baule War Cemetery
1 G 17

J Douglas Glennie
Rev.
R.A. Ch.D.
30 September 1940
Stirling (Mar Place) Cemetery
Compt. H 8

John B M Gordon
Sgt Met/Observer
R.A.F.
1944

Alistair Gove
Ord. Seaman
R.N.
25 February 1944
Plymouth Naval Memorial
88 1

Alexander Gray
Sgt Air Bomber
R.A.F.
2 February 1945
Springbank Cemetery, Aberdeen

Charles W G Gray
F.O.
R.A.F.V.R.
14 April 1943
Edinburgh (Warriston)
Crematorium
Pan 2

George Green
Flt Eng.
R.A.F. (Bomber Command)
1943

Laurence H Gruer
Sgt
R.A.F.
30 July 1941
Runnymede Memorial
Pan 44

Alexander G Harvery
Sgt
R.A.F.
15 March 1942
Runnymede Memorial
Pan 85

Thomas B T Hendry
L. Cpl
Int. Corps
21 June 1944
Delhi War Cemetery
1 G 3

Gordon Hill
Capt.
R.E.
1942

Alexander Hunter
Capt.
R.E.
20 December 1942
Singapore Memorial
Col. 37

Frederick Hunter
Capt.
Indian Medical Service
22 January 1943
Kirkee War Cemetery
13 D 10

James W Hutton
Engineering Off.
Merchant Navy
17 March 1942
Tower Hill Memorial
Pan 94

John C Innes, O.B.E.
February 1943
M.V. "Henry Stanley"

Alexander l Johnston
F.O.
R.A.F.
13 September 1944
Malta Memorial
Pan 13 Col. 1

William H Jupp
Rifleman
K.R.R.C.
31 August 1942
El Alamein War Cemetery
XXVII G 10

John F Kelman
W.O. Pilot
R.A.F.
14 February 1945
The Hague (Westduin) General
Cemetery
Allied Plot 5 93

James G Kerr
Apprentice
Merchant Marine
14 February 1940
Tower Hill Memorial
Pan 108

Sydney Laing
Aircraftsman
R.A.F.
6 March 1942
Singapore Memorial
Col. 418

Donald Law
F.O.
R.A.F.V.R.
3 March 1945
Springbank Cemetery, Aberdeen
Sec. T, Grave 182

William Lawson
L. Ac.
R.A.F.
7 November 1944
Runnymede Memorial
Pan 242

Douglas M Leitch
FltLt
R.A.F.
6 March 1945
Ravenna War Cemetery
I G 24

William J Lewis
P.O.
R.A.F.V.R.
16 March 1942
Springbank Cemetery, Aberdeen
Sec. T, Grave 192

William J Lunan
Lt
Gurkha Rifles
6 December 1942
Karachi War Cemetery
9 A 1

Iain R Macaulay
F.O.
R.A.F.
15 November 1944
Runnymede Memorial

George M McBain
Cpl
Malayan Defence Corps
September 1943
Kanchanaburi War Cemetery
2 Q 19

Alastair D MacDonald
Lt
Royal Norfolk Regt
28 February 1942
Singapore Memorial
Col. 47

Charles A MacGregor
Capt.
Black Watch (R.H.R.)
27 October 1942
El Alamein War Cemetery
V E 9

John F McHugh
Flt Sgt
R.A.F.
13 July 1944
Giey-sur-Aujon Churchyard

John S McKay
Flt Sgt
R.A.F.
25 October 1943
Runnymede Memorial
Pan 137

Norman W M MacKenzie
Flt Sgt
R.A.F.
6 October 1945
Singapore Memorial
Col. 450

Kenneth G MacLery
Sgt Obs
R.A.F.
July 1941

William T McLennan
Sgt
R.A.F.
8 January 1943
Vorden General Cemetery
Grave 7

Ian N MacPherson
Pte
R.A.O.C.
21 May 1944
Lochalsh Churchyard
Grave 201

George McWilliam
Pte
F.M.S. Volunteer Force
6 June 1945
Kanchanaburi War Cemetery
6 E 14

James A Manson
P.O.
R.A.F.
26 August 1942
Brookwood Military Cemetery
22 A 5

William A Manson
Bdr
R.F.A.
22 February 1945
Mook War Cemetery
II A 12

Stanley A Marr
Flt Sgt
R.A.F.
5 June 1942
Bergen General Cemetery
1 C 7

Alexander Mathieson
Sqn Ldr
R.A.F.V.R.
8 September 1941
Runnymede Memorial
Pan 28

Norman A Mercer
Flt Sgt
R.A.F.
25 October 1942
Nant-le-Grand Communal
Cemetery
Grave 2

James J Michie
Tpr
RAC
14 September 1944
Gradara War Cemetery
I B 29

Eric C Middleton
Capt.
Merchant Navy
17 November 1939
Tower Hill Memorial
Pan 79

John M D Middleton
2nd Eng. Off.
Merchant Navy
5 August 1942
Tower Hill Memorial
Pan 10

Angus M Milne
Flt Sgt
7 September 1942
Reichswald Forest War Cemetery
16 G 11

Charles M Milne
Capt.
Merchant Navy
16 September 1939
Calais Souther Cemetery
J 2

Douglas B Milne
Cpl
R.A.F.V.R.
19 December 1942
Sydney War Cemetery
2Z C 1

George K T Milne
P.O.
R.A.F.
6 February 1942
Runnymede Memorial
Pan 70

Andrew J Mitchell
Sgt.
R.A.F.
27 April 1944
Malta Memorial
Pan 15 Col. 1

Anthony G L Mitchell
Sgt Observer
R.A.F.
July 1941
Runnymede Memorial
Pan 48

Charles Mitchell
F.O.
R.A.F.
9 November 1942
Hamburg Cemetery
8A C 1-15

Edward Mitchell
First Officer
Merchant Navy
9 June 1941
Tower Hill Memorial
Pan 97

William M Moir
2/Lt
Burma Rifles
4 March 1942
Rangoon Memorial
Face 19

Norman Moodie
Sgt
London Scottish
19 February 1944
Beach Head War Cemetery, Anzio
IX D 10

Walter Morrice
F.O.
R.A.F.
9 November 1944
Allenvale Cemetery, Aberdeen
Sec. Y, Grave 185

George C Morrison
Sub Lt
Fleet Air Arm R.N.V.R.
5 June 1942
Methlick Cemetery
Sec. I, Row 10, Grave 30

Alexander E Mulholland
F.O.
R.A.F.
21 December 1942
Geraardsbergen Communal
Cemetery
06-Sep

William A H Munro, M.C.
Capt.
R.T.R.
5 June 1945
Taukkyan War Cemetery
20 E 13

John Murray
Lt
R.A.
11 July 1944
Tilly-sur-Seulles War Cemetery
VII A 12

Henry J M Mutch, M.C.
Lt
R.E.
4 October 1947

James S Nairn
2/Lt
R.E.
17 December 1941
Grove Cemetery, Aberdeen
Grave 894

William Newton
Lt Eng.
Merchant Navy
5 November 1940
Liverpool Naval Memorial
Pan. 2 Col. 2

Nelson D Ogg
Sig.
R.C. of Signals
15 March 1943
Prague War Cemetery
IV C 12

Edward J Ogilvie
Spr
R.E.
16 October 1942
El Alamein War Cemetery
III C 25

George Okada
Pte
Royal Scots
3 November 1944

Alexander Philip
Capt.
R.A.
3 April 1942
Perth War Cemetery
P B 9

Charles A Philip
Sgt
F.M.S. Rifle Reserve
20 September 1943
Thanbyuzayat War Cemetery
B6 G 13

George R Pirie
Air Gunner
R.A.F.
22 May 1940
Haucourt Communal Cemetery,
Pas de Calais

Ian Prosser
P.O.
R.A.F.
28 October 1940
Great Bircham (St Mary)
Churchyard
1 1 11

Forbes G Rae
Sgt
R.A.F.
3 November 1941
Runnymede Memorial
Pan. 50

William F Raffan
P.O.
R.A.F.
29 October 1942
Taule Communal Memorial
Grave 6

Archie Reid
Sqn Ldr
R.A.F.
17 July 1946
Aberdeen Crematorium

Ronald S Richmond
Sgt
R.A.F.
30 May 1943
Reichswald Forest War
Cemetery
5 E 12

James R Ritchie
Flt Lt
R.A.F.
4 January 1943
Heliopolis War Cemetery
3 H 25

Hector Robertson
F.O.
R.A.F.
10 April 1943
Oudewater Protestant Cemetery
6 67

John K Robertson
Sgt
R.A.F.
26 November 1943
Heverlee War Cemetery
2 A 3

Leslie Robertson, M.C.
Capt.
King's African Rifles
7 December 1944
Taukkyan War Cemetery
16A F 19

Alistair W Robson
P.O.
R.A.F.
12 June 1941
Runnymede Memorial
Pan. 34

John A Rose
Sig.
R.C. of Signals
22 April 1944
Ramleh War Cemetery
5 B 19

David A Sadler
P.O.
R.A.F.
24 August 1940
Grove Cemetery, Aberdeen
Grave 196

James S Salmond
Sgt. Radio Obs.
R.A.F.
9 April 1942
Springbank Cemetery, Aberdeen
Sec. E, Grave 534

James J M Saunders
F.O.
R.A.F.V.R.
22 September 1944
Springbank Cemetery, Aberdeen
Sec. U, Grave 367

Ian D Singer
Sgt Pilot
R.A.F.
1 August 1942
Jonkerbos War Cemetery
12 1 2

Walter J Donald Smith
Sgt
R.A.F.
5 September 1944
Alamein Memorial
Col. 280

Edward W Spiller
Flt Sgt
R.A.F.V.R.
2 July 1942
Alamein Memorial
Col. 262

Leslie F Steele
Sgt
R.A.F., W. Op. and Air Gunner
26 March 1941
Runnymede Memorial
Pan. 52

Ian C Stephen
Capt.
R.A.M.C.
8 May 1944

Kenneth R Still
Sgt (Flt Eng.)
R.A.F.
5/6 March 1945
Durnbach War Cemetery
11 E 7

Charles S M Thom
L. Cpl
Hong Kong Volunteer Defence
Corps
25 December 1941
Sai Wan Memorial
Col. 33

William M Tullett
F.O.
R.A.F.
18 February 1945
Madras War Cemetery, Chennai
1 K 13

David R Wallace
F.O.
R.A.F.
4 November 1944
Arnhem Oosterbeek War Cemetery
4 D 3

George J Wright
L. Ac.
R.A.F.
27 June 1942
Allenvale Cemetery, Aberdeen
Sec. C, Grave 277

DECORATIONS:
THE SECOND WORLD WAR

Angus	Warrant Bomb. Alexander R	Member of the Order of the British Empire, Military Cross
Argo	Lt Col G A E	Military Cross
Blacklaw	James S	Military Medal
Bowman	Maj. Francis J S	Member of the Order of the British Empire
Brockie	Capt. A J W	Military Cross
Burnett	Capt. William R B	Member of the Order of the British Empire
Cable	Capt. Harry S	Military Medal, Military Cross
Cameron	Capt. William J	Mentioned in Dispatches
Chalmers	F.O. Christopher W	Distinguished Flying Medal, Distinguished Flying Cross
Clark	Flt Sgt Gilbert G C	British Empire Medal
Craig	Capt. Norman J	Military Cross
Croil	Air Vice Marshal George	Air Force Cross, Croix de Guerre
Crow	F.O. Henry J	Distinguished Flying Cross
Cumming	Wg. Cdr. J C	Mentioned in Dispatches
Davidson	Chief Eng. John H	Officer of the Order of the British Empire
Dawson	James A	Commander of the Order of the British Empire
Dean	George C	Member of the Order of the British Empire
Donald	Charles	Officer of the Order of the British Empire
Ellis	F.O. Walter D	Croix de Guerre
Findlay	Capt. James	Distinguished Service Order

Forbes	Flt. Lt. Cameron M	Distinguished Flying Cross
Fox	Douglas P	Distinguished Flying Cross and Bar
Frain	Flt. Lt. George	Member of the Order of the British Empire, Mentioned in Dispatches
Fraser	Senior Chaplain The Rev. Col Alan J	Twice Mentioned in Dispatches
Fraser	Warrant Officer Alexander C	Distinguished Flying Cross
Gall	Lt. Herbert McR	Military Cross
Gervaise	Lt. Walter A	Distinguished Service Cross, Croix de Guerre
Gill	Capt. Samuel M.	Mentioned in Dispatches
Gordon	Warrant Officer William J	Distinguished Flying Cross
Grant	The Rev. Joseph	Military Cross
Green	Flt. Sgt. Alexander	Mentioned in Dispatches
Guyan	Warrant Officer Samuel	Distinguished Flying Cross
Hogg	Capt. James C	Military Cross and Bar
Ingram	Telegraphist James	Mentioned in Dispatches
Innes	John Charles	Officer of the Order of the British Empire
Lakin	Maj. Edward D	Member of the Order of the British Empire
Levack	Col. David P	Commander of the Order of the British Empire, Territorial Efficiency Decoration
Low	Capt. Edward O	Mentioned in Dispatches
MacFarlane	Paymaster Lt. Donald S	Distinguished Service Cross
MacKenzie	Lt. Col. Ian	Distinguished Service Order
McConnach	Chief Constable James	King's Police Medal
McKiddie	Maj. John M	Mentioned in Dispatches
McRobert	Col. George R	Knighthood
McWilliam	The Rev. Keith	Territorial Efficiency Decoration
Millar	P.O. Andrew	Distinguished Flying Cross
Milne	Flt. Lt. Evander M M	Distinguished Flying Cross
Moir	Pte. Robert G D	Military Medal
Munro	Capt. William	Military Cross
Mutch	Lt. Henry	Military Cross

Newton	Flt. Sgt. Robert	Distinguished Flying Medal
Pirie	Flt. Sgt. Richard T	Distinguished Flying Medal
Rae	2/Lt.	Commended for Gallantry
Readhead	Flt. Lt. William F	Distinguished Flying Cross
Reid	P.O. Harry S	Distinguished Flying Cross
Rix	Sgt. Archibald J	Distinguished Flying Medal
Robb	P.O. John W	Distinguished Flying Cross
Robertson	Capt. Leslie	Military Cross
Shearer	Capt. Duncan G	Military Cross
Shearer	Lt. David H	Commended by Commander-in-Chief, India
Simpson	John Alexander	Companion of the Most Ancient Order of the British Empire
Souter	Surgeon Captain James C	King Haakon V11 Liberty Cross
Stark	Maj. W J K	Officer of the Order of the British Empire
Stewart	Captain Walter, M B Ch B	Member of the British Empire
Still	Sub Lt. William J S	Mentioned in Dispatches
Sutherland	Flight Officer Huistean	Distinguished Flying Cross
Swapp	Surgeon Lt Commander Garden H	Distinguished Service Cross
Tawse	Chief Eng. Officer William	Officer of the Order of the British Empire
Thomson	Acting Wg. Cdr. Ronald Bain	Distinguished Service Order, Distinguished Flying Cross
Thomson	Capt. James I F	Member of the Order of the British Empire
Thomson	Flt. Sgt. Ian M.	Distinguished Flying Medal
Wetherly	Skipper	Officer of the Order of the British Empire
Wishart	F.O. Robert W	Distinguished Flying Cross
Wood	John Calder	Military Cross, Officer of the Order of the British Empire

PART TWO

THE COMBINED CADET FORCE
AND PIPE BAND

Chapter Eight

THE COMBINED CADET FORCE

In 1948 it was decided to combine all school-based cadet units into one organization to be known as the Combined Cadet Force. Initially, 247 schools accepted the invitation to adopt the new scheme and the new C.C.F. was honoured by H.M. King George VI becoming C.C.F. Captain-General (a position held today by Her Majesty the Queen). Officers were frequently members of the teaching staff returning to peacetime employment following service in the Armed Forces during the war.

The Combined Cadet Force is administered by the Ministry of Defence, although an individual school's C.C.F. activities are subject to the policy of the Headmaster. It is a voluntary, part-time organization in schools which are mostly but not exclusively in the independent sector. The organization is based on the contingent, which may consist of Army, Royal Air Force, Royal Navy and Royal Marines sections. There are currently 253 schools with Combined Cadet Force contingents. This is a number slightly larger than the number of schools in 1948 and it is interesting to note that interest has been sustained over the sixty years of the modern C.C.F. There are some 1,800 C.C.F. officers and 42,000 cadets across the UK.

The emphasis is on the *partnership* between the military authorities and the school. The M.o.D. provides training and remuneration for adult volunteers, access to military facilities, training assistance, access to military transport, uniforms, weapons, ammunition and various stores and equipment. In return, participating schools undertake to provide adult volunteers, time within and outwith the school day (provided by both adults and cadets), accommodation, storage and administrative and other support.

The purpose of Combined Cadet Force training is to develop powers of leadership and the personal qualities outlined in the aims of the organization: responsibility, self-reliance, resourcefulness, endurance and perseverance and most of all, a sense of service to the community. Crucial to the thinking behind the existence of the C.C.F. is that such qualities, whilst important to each member of the Armed Forces, are equally important to "the civil life of the nation" as stated in the Aims of the C.C.F.

The C.C.F. continues to play a major role in the life of Robert Gordon's College as one of the leading extra-curricular activities. Many Gordonians have gone on to highly successful military careers following membership of the C.C.F. whilst at school. It is however fully acknowledged that only a minority of cadets will wish to follow this path, and this is reflected in the training offered to pupils in S2 and above. Skills developed through membership are highly valued in all walks of life, and this is recognised by pupils, parents, universities and future employers. In addition to formal military and leadership training, cadets have the potential to enjoy a wealth of opportunities. Recently, cadets have for example participated in visits abroad, sailing, wind surfing, cross-country skiing, hill walking, white-water rafting, kayaking, abseiling and parachuting. This is in addition to more routine activities including visits, shooting, flying and gliding. Membership is open to both boys and girls, and indeed many girls have enjoyed a long and successful connection with the C.C.F. and have held the most senior positions.

A team of officers from the teaching staff (commissioned in the Territorial Army or the Royal Air Force Volunteer Reserve Training branch as appropriate) leads the venture, committed to the training and opportunities made possible through partnership with the military authorities. This is a partnership which adds greatly to the wider educational provision offered by the College.

Equally important are the senior cadets who act as non-commissioned officers. Time and time again it is stressed to these young people that they hold key positions within the C.C.F. The unit is of course deliberately structured to ensure that at an early stage, senior cadets are placed in positions of authority through which they are able to develop leadership qualities and gain experience of responsibility. Many aspects of the training of younger cadets are led by them and staff depend of them for much of the administration and organization of the unit, particularly at camp. Throughout the history of the unit in our school we have been able to rely on the integrity, high standards and willingness to learn of countless young people. Without them, the unit would not be the success it is today.

Chapter Nine

THE ARMY SECTION

The military aspects of Army Section training provide an introduction to skills associated with Army officer training at the Royal Military Academy Sandhurst. Cadets progress through a comprehensive syllabus of training leading to advanced awards including aspects such as fieldcraft, skill at arms, signalling and infantry tactics, navigation, drill, turn out, First Aid, map & compass, shooting, sports, A.T. camps and leadership.

The Army Section of the C.C.F. has enjoyed a long and highly successful history in R.G.C., whose Army cadets were some of the earliest UK C.C.F. members. The first Contingent Commander was Captain Murdo McRae of the Modern Languages department, supported by Robert Mowatt, Brian Ludwig and James Geals.

Until the late Fifties C.C.F. training was purely military in nature and included drill, battle craft, fieldcraft, map reading, shooting skills and handling of weapons. In 1950 the shooting team won the Tawse Shooting Trophy for all cadet companies in North East Scotland. Training Proficiency Tests were held and a high standard has been consistent over the years. At one stage R.G.C. had a record number of entrants to the Army College at Wellbeck Abbey. (Most recently, Daniel Tope was accepted for Wellbeck in 2001.)

From 1958 the C.C.F. was to receive less assistance from the Army. Former Contingent Commander Major John Dow M.B.E. recalls:

Flt. Lt. Greg House, Falkland Islands, March 2008

Tornado F3s of XXV(F) Sqn flown by Sq. Ldr. Nick Gatenby and (nearest to camera) Flt. Lt. Greg House
Photograph: Geoffrey Lee, Planefocus Ltd.

The Hospital Drum of 1835, played at various official functions throughout the city including the opening of Duthie Park, Victoria Docks and the New Market.

Pipe Band 1949-50
Front Row left to right: Pipe Sgt. Kenneth Melvin, Ian. MacKenzie, Alan Anderson, Pipe Major Alistair Gunn, Norman Mathieson, Ian MacLellan, W. Anderson
Rear Row: Drum Sgt. John Runcie, William Pardon, Jock Mitchell, Ian "Pop" Macauley, James Hunter, Bertie Greig, James Couper, J. MacKenzie

R.G.C. with Aberdeen University O.T.C. pipers at the Coronation Parade, Union St. 1952
Alex Urquhart is 2nd from front as Junior Drum Major.
Photograph: Aberdeen Journals Ltd.

Pipe Band at Seafield 1953/4
Band includes Drum Major Alex Urquhart (far left N.B. position of mace), Pipe Major Ian MacKenzie, Kenneth Muirhead, G. W. Whyte, Brian McCulloch, Drum Sgt. "Jock" Mitchell, William Blacklaw, John Allan, Tom Simpson, Bert Greig and William Brandie.
Photograph: Aberdeen Journals Ltd.

Left: Drummer A. Cruickshank meets Brigadier J.F. Macnab at Bridge of Don Barracks 1952/53
Photograph: Aberdeen Journals Ltd.

Left: Pipe Major Ramsay A. Urquhart 1981-83
Below: 250th Anniversary Pipe Band 2000

Drum Major Douglas Bennett and Pipe Major Bill Fraser 1960-61

Pipe Major Fraser Maitland 2004
Top right: Pipe Major Andrew MacMillan 2000
Above right: 2007 – 08 Pipe Major Ewan Robertson displaying the 1946-2006 anniversary banner gifted by founding and former members

R.G.C. Band playing during H.M. The Queen's Jubilee celebrations, Union St. 2002

There was a change in emphasis towards less formal training with fewer tactical exercises. Certificate A was replaced by the Basic and Proficiency Tests, which are terms still in use today. A new activity, Adventure or Arduous Training, became very popular and numbers increased. These Arduous Training programmes took cadets and staff into the hills for four-day exercises, often under canvas. In October and at Easter they would set out to Derry Lodge, Glen Dall, Rothiemurcus or elsewhere, and all at the Army's expense. "Compo" rations were popular and activities were frequently "adventurous" in ways which would not pass the scrutiny of the risk assessments of the twenty-first century! Character-building sorties were demanding and testing for those displaying leadership qualities. Officers went on mountain leadership courses to qualify as instructors in various mountain skills. Activities were imaginative and included overnights in the mountains, flights in a barrage balloon and abseiling – including once over the clock-face at Seafield and, later, down the outside wall of the R.G.C. Science Block.

The Cadet Training Centre, Frimley Park, opened in 1959 and is the venue for training courses for all Army Cadet Force and C.C.F. (Army Section) officers. Frimley is also well known to many of our cadets (both Army and R.A.F.) who have attended the Cadet Leadership Course over the years.

1960 saw the centenary of the Cadet Force movement. Two senior cadets attended the Centenary Parade at Buckingham Palace. A record was presented to the Captain General, Her Majesty The Queen, at the parade on Friday 22nd July 1960 on behalf of each UK school and Combined Cadet Force Contingent. The R.G.C. page devised for this document is reproduced in this work.

An innovation in 1961 saw the C.C.F. forming the Guard of Honour at Founder's Day. Also introduced was the naming of platoons after Gordon Highlanders' battle honours Anzio, Tel el Kebir and Alamein. The same year, the first two cadets attended the Joint Services Cadet Badge Tests at Frimley Park.

There was great excitement in the College on 3rd March 1966 with the arrival of a Wessex helicopter from H.M.S. *Condor*, Arbroath, in the front quad. Officers from the Fleet Air Arm Presentation Team showed the aircraft to senior pupils and staff and gave illustrated talks to over 200 pupils on careers as helicopter, Buccaneer and Vixen aircrew in the Fleet Air Arm.

A highlight of the cadet year has always been the Annual Camp when, in early years as now, about eighty per cent of Army Section cadets would attend. This was generally held at the C.C.F. Central Camp Cultybraggan, near Comrie in Perthshire. Cultybraggan was built in 1941 as a labour camp for Italian prisoners of war and later became a transit camp for German prisoners. It housed up to 4,000 prisoners including the ringleaders of the Devizes plot which aimed to mount an insurrection from within the country through the release of some 250,000 prisoners of war. Cultybraggan also held, for a time, Rudolph Hess, Hitler's deputy, after he parachuted from his Me. 110 aircraft near Glasgow on 10th May 1941 on his "peace mission" to see the Duke of Hamilton, whom he had met at the time of the Berlin Olympics in 1936. After the war, the camp hosted cadet camps by schools and units all over the UK for many years. It was an ideal location for service training with hills, rivers, forests, shooting ranges and assault courses providing experience of a week of Army life. Of note was the fact that Cadet Andrew Krebs attended Summer Camp at Cultybraggan as a cadet in the 1990s, his grandfather having been a German prisoner there during the war.

Visits were not confined to Perthshire. Even in the early years, camps were held at a fascinating range of venues including Garelochhead, Fort George, Barry Buddon, Inverness, Troon,

Glencorse, Ayrshire, Applecross, Aultbea, Skye and, on more than one occasion, Orkney. It is noted perhaps with some regret that only during one year in three were the cadets permitted to camp "furth of Scotland", but camps were nevertheless held in locations such as Strensall (Yorkshire), Ballykinlar (Ireland), Aldershot and Warcop (Cumbria). The new facility at Barry Buddon, Carnoustie, with first-class training facilities and accommodation, continues to offer tremendous opportunities to the cadets of the twenty-first century.

Cadets have travelled abroad on many occasions. Many cadets have been fortunate to be allocated a camp in Germany. One of the first of these was over Easter 1953, when twenty-two cadets and three officers were guests of the 2nd Battalion, The Black Watch, in Dusseldorf. In a very full programme of activities, cadets experienced sailing on the Rhine on a German Air Sea Rescue craft and saw German wartime defences at first hand. Subsequent visits included Minden with 1st Battalion, The Cameronians, in 1963, Münster in 1973 and Hemer in 1973. There have also been camps at Soltain (near Belsen) and R.A.F. Wildenwrath near the Dutch border. Captain Andrew Hopps accompanied two cadets, Cpls Derek Neilson and Stewart Bremner, on the Joint Services Camp at Gibraltar in 1989 hosted by the Royal Green Jackets. This camp involved 100 cadets and ten officers from units from all parts of the UK Summer 2004 saw the re-introduction of a programme of visits to Germany and R.G.C. was selected as one of the first schools to benefit. Twenty cadets and four officers under the Army Section Commander, Captain Chris Spracklin, participated in a visit to Hameln hosted by the 28th Royal Engineers. Cadets travelled to Germany again in 2005 as guests of the Royal Logistics Corps and enjoyed a very full week of activities, including sailing on the Möhne Dam and a very moving visit to the site of the former Bergen-Belsen Concentration Camp.

In session 1988–89 Cadet Scott Lindsay excelled himself by

gaining one of only twelve places on a six-week UK/Canada exchange to Whitehorse in the Yukon and leading the passing-out parade at the end of the course as Best Cadet. Col. Sgt Emma Anderson was one of the twelve UK cadets selected for the exchange in 1994, taking part in the National Army Cadet Camp, Banff, British Columbia. The only successful Scottish C.C.F. candidate, Col. Sgt Ross Melton, won through against very stiff competition to the very last round of selection to undertake six weeks of adventurous training activities in Canada in 2005. Although he was disappointed not to be picked, this nevertheless represented a tremendous achievement.

Enthusiasm continued throughout the 1980s and 1990s. Annual reports in the *Gordonian* by writers such as C.S.M. Nicholas Duckworth, C.S.M. Gregg Wilkie, R.S.M. Andrew Reid, Sgt Nils Reid and C.S.M. Lucy Rennie outline activities and achievements and, without exception, acknowledge the debt owed by cadets to enthusiastic and selfless members of staff. As one example, it was customary during this period to run a C.C.F. residential project as part of the S5 post-examination Projects' Week. The 1994 *Gordonian* included a report on one such week by future Otaki Scholar (and later Royal Marines officer) Anthony Liva:

> After a long and hard drive we fell gasping out of the hot, dusty coach at the Linn of Dee. However this was not to be our final destination, which lay at the far end of the Lairig Ghru. [During the week] we climbed the Devil's Point, Cairn Toul, Angel's Peak, Einich Cairn and Braeraich.
>
> Thanks for this excellent, invigorating and educational week must not only go to Capt. Cowie and Lt. Ramsay for organising it but also to Maj. Dow for his appetisingly good cooking, not to mention his barbecue which will be kept warm in the memory of the cadets during many a hungry moment. (p.75)

The Nijmegen Marches

Mention must be made of one particular event in Holland, in which the College on one occasion (1987) represented the Scottish cadets. The Nijmegen Marches originated in 1909 with Dutch military efforts to increase the long-distance marching and weight-carrying ability of infantry soldiers, and eventually evolved into a prestigious international competition. The four-day march is held annually and is centred around Holland's oldest town, Nijmegen. The event involves four consecutive days of marching a distance of 25–30 miles. The town hosts a huge festival before, during and after the event, which is approaching its 100th anniversary. The only breaks have been for the two world wars. It attracts over 40,000 entrants along with tens of thousands of spectators. Individuals, civilian groups, police/ emergency services, military and cadet teams from all over the world participate. Of the twelve cadets who repre-sented R.G.C. three became serving officers – Major Cameron Humphries and Major Ronnie Coutts (The Highlanders/Royal Regiment of Scotland) and Captain Stuart Nicol (The Argyll and Sutherland Highlanders). The Gordonian C.C.F. article of 1987 makes interesting reading:

We were based at Humersood Camp with 800 military personnel. An early start, 4.30 in the morning, gave us the cool of the day for most of the (25-mile) march and with occasional rests for nourishment and medical aid we completed the day with sore feet and very tired. However the spirit was good and determin-ation to make a good account of ourselves prevailed and the marches continued for a further 3 days until we completed the distance. On the last day, 5 miles short of the town, we changed into kilts for the final 'march in' through the festival town which was bedecked with flags and bunting for the occasion. Everyone in the town turned out to watch the closing stages and we were embarrassingly presented with bouquets of flowers by many of the spectators. Perhaps the kilts had something to do with that. This was indeed an arduous and very exhausting achievement which certainly will not be forgotten by the cadets who took part. (p.54)

Flt Lt Neil Johnson was present at the event in July 2007 and it has been proposed that cadets might participate again in the future.

In April 2004 the three platoons in the Army Section were renamed the Gordons, the Seaforths and the Camerons after the three regiments which were amalgamated into The Highlanders. 2004 saw the retirement from the teaching staff of previous Contingent Commander Bruce Simms and Headmaster Brian Lockhart, both of whom had taken a keen interest in the activities of the C.C.F. On his retirement, Mr Lockhart kindly presented a trophy to the C.C.F. to be awarded to a leading Army Section cadet on an annual basis.

The Royal Regiment of Scotland

With the demise of the Gordon Highlanders, a Beating Retreat and Re-badging ceremony was held in front of the Auld Hoose on 30th March 2000. Col. Sgt Alysha Whyte was presented with the new cap badge of The Highlanders by Brigadier Simon Allen, Commanding Officer of 51 (Scottish) Brigade. Guests included Lieutenant General Sir Peter Graham, last Colonel of the Gordon Highlanders, and Col. Alistair Cumming, Secretary of The Highlanders.

In an event similar to that in 2000, a re-badging ceremony was held on 6th November 2007 when the unit adopted the cap badge of the Royal Regiment of Scotland. This marked the conversion of The Highlanders into a battalion within the newly formed Royal Regiment. The badge was presented to C.S.M. Callum Nixon by Lt Col A.R. Cram T.D. in the presence of parents, senior staff, representatives of the new regiment and distinguished guests.

These were occasions which provided the opportunity to look to the future under new cap badges whilst celebrating the association of the College with the great traditions of both the Gordon Highlanders and The Highlanders over many years.

Army Section Officers

One of the best-known C.C.F. figures in the College, Major John Dow, commanded the unit from 1960 to 1989, not missing a single annual camp. He was awarded the M.B.E. for services to the Cadet Forces in 1982. Major Dow's contribution to the development of the contingent was immense, and former pupils visiting the school and discussing the C.C.F. invariably recall his tremendous drive, enthusiasm and passion for the very many activities in which he was involved. John came to Gordon's in 1952 following National Service as a Physical Training Instructor with the Royal Engineers. He remained a regular at games afternoons at Countesswells for many years after his official retirement from the P.E. Department in 1988 and is known to generations of Gordonians as one of the stalwarts of the P.E. Department. A Division 1 referee in National Leagues, he twice ran the touch for internationals at Murrayfield.

Summer Camp 1986 was typical of John's imaginative approach, with the contingent occupying the former gun battery at Stromness, overlooking Scapa Flow. John was at the time Housemaster of Sillerton House (a post he held for fifteen years), and his wife May oversaw all catering arrangements for the week. In addition to normal cadet activities, the boys visited St Magnus Cathedral, Kirkwall and Scara Brae, and walked across Hoy to the Old Man with full waterproof gear but in blistering heat, camping on the island thereafter "where the diplomacy of Captain Simms in his negotiation with the officials of the R.S.P.B. ensured that good "bivvy" sites were found despite new restrictions on the island" (*Gordonian* 1987 p.54). In practice this meant that Captain Simms, in a state of complete exhaustion, sat down at the end of the march and refused to move one step more. This is an experience the author has never forgotten! On his retirement from both the C.C.F. and College staff in 1988, John Dow was presented with a very fine portrait of himself by Art Department colleague Tom Hendry.

Many of the other Gordon's staff "characters" were associated with the C.C.F. at one time or another. "Lifer" John Gordon attended the school as a pupil before completing National Service with the Royal Army Education Corps. Before becoming Deputy Head (a post he held for sixteen years), John was deeply involved in extra-curricular activities. He served in the C.C.F. for twenty years and was committed to the development of the organization. Captain Tom Collins, the former Head of the R.E. Department, served for some twenty-five years, including commanding the unit at one point. He was well known for his orienteering and cross-country skiing interests. John Jermieson assisted with administration for some time. Major Bruce Simms (mentioned above) was involved for some twenty years, commanding the unit for eight years until 1997. Quoted in the *Gordonian* article marking his retirement from the post of Head of Biology in 2004, he stated that "good should be done by stealth and not in a blaze of glory" (p.11) and he led by example. Under his guidance the R.A.F. Section was founded in 1994 and he oversaw the development of music through the Pipe Band. The C.C.F. was only one of a number of activities in which he was involved and he added greatly to the wider life of the school. Responsible for R.G.C. Cubs, Scouts and Venture Scouts, he was for a time District Commissioner of Scouts. For many years Assistant Housemaster to John Dow at Sillerton House, he was also a leading figure in the Duke of Edinburgh's Award Scheme. Known widely as a "bon viveur and sportsman" (again from the *Gordonian*), his influence is still felt in the C.C.F. today.

More recently, Major Kevin Cowie (currently Principal Teacher, Guidance), and Captain Andrew Hopps (currently Head of Art), served for eighteen and fourteen years respectively. Along with several of their predecessors, Major Cowie and Captain Hopps were awarded the Cadet Forces Medal for "long and meritorious service to the Cadet Forces". Their interest in C.C.F. activities continues and their contribution was crucial to the success of the contingent as it exists today. Other noted officers have included Malcolm Hicks, Bill Currie, Fred Skinner, Alex Gardner, Steven Cardno, Margaret Ramsay and David Strang, the current Head of Biology.

The section continues to thrive and enjoy success today with some 120 active members, commanded by 2i/c the Contingent Major Chris Spracklin and very ably assisted by Captain Mike Maitland, Captain David Morris and Lt Kirsten Hastie.

Chapter Ten

THE ROYAL AIR FORCE SECTION

A major development took place in 1994 with the establishment of a Royal Air Force Section by the present Contingent Commander, Squadron Leader Daniel Montgomery, to complement training and activities offered by the Army Section. This brought R.A.F. cadets back to the College after an absence of almost fifty years. The section has attracted interest from an additional selection of pupils and parents, naturally including those with an interest in aviation.

Training in the R.A.F. Section is broadly similar to Army Section training with the emphasis on preparing senior cadets to assume a high degree of responsibility for their younger colleagues at an early stage.

Cadets progress through a flexible training syllabus which includes dress, turnout, recognition of badges of rank, shooting, R.A.F. knowledge, aircraft recognition and the academic study of aviation subjects such as rules of the air, propulsion, navigation and principles of flight. In senior years, cadets are given the opportunity to specialise. The three elements of the Advanced Badge include the study of one of the subjects above, development of a skill, interest or adventurous training activity (in much the same way as a Duke of Edinburgh's Award candidate) and reaching a satisfactory standard in terms of leadership training and experience. Remaining time is allocated to activities such as the construction of a flight simulator which is an ongoing project at the time of writing.

From the outset, R.A.F. Section activities such as Air Experience Flying in the de Havilland Chipmunk aircraft at

R.A.F. Turnhouse proved to be extremely popular before the move first to the Scottish Aviation Bulldog and now the Grob Tutor at R.A.F. Leuchars. Each cadet is entitled to at least one Air Experience flight per year in the dual control Tutor aircraft (whether they prefer sightseeing over the Tay or Forth Bridges or having the opportunity to experience aerobatics) and cadets also undertake gliding training in the Viking glider. In both activities, even the youngest cadets are encouraged to take control of the aircraft at an early stage. Cadets are eligible for participation in annual camps at front-line Royal Air Force stations and also camps abroad. Members have enjoyed twenty Easter and Summer camps. There have also been visits to a wide selection of establishments including R.A.F. Cranwell, Kinloss, Leuchars, Coltishall, Wittering, Conningsby, Northolt, Uxbridge and Valley. Many cadets have successfully completed camps abroad including R.A.F. Bruggen and other bases in Germany as well as on Cyprus. Others have enjoyed overseas flights. Camps also provide the opportunity to fly in aircraft operated at the base. Flights in helicopters, training aircraft, transport aircraft and tankers have all been provided. On one occasion the highlight of the week was observing air-to-air refuelling of a Jaguar aircraft by the tanker in which the cadets were flying. Each camp programme includes a cultural visit to the local town or city and over the years cadets have visited London, Windsor, Oxford, Cambridge, Bath, Chester, Cardiff, Edinburgh and many other cities. We did however disappoint one Air Cadet Liaison Officer at R.A.F. Buchan who had planned, as the highlight of the camp, a tour of Aberdeen.

Scholarships in both powered flying and gliding are available to senior cadets who show determination and aptitude. Gliding scholarships can lead to a solo flight and the award of gliding wings. The Air Cadet Pilot Navigation Training Scheme also provides a two-week course to selected cadets. The International Air Cadet Exchange programme is open to S6

cadets whilst others in S4 and in S5 are encouraged to partici-
pate in the Air Cadet Leadership Course at the R.A.F. College
Cranwell and the Cadet Leadership Course at Frimley Park.
Cadets are entitled to attend courses at the two Air Cadet
Adventurous Training Centres, Windermere in Cumbria and
Llanbedr in Wales. Many cadets have taken advantage of these
opportunities over the years.

1995 saw the demise of the C.C.F. R.A.F. Section at Aberdeen
Grammar School, and left R.G.C. as the only UK C.C.F. R.A.F.
Section north of Perthshire. The Grammar School's loss was
our gain, and R.G.C. was very fortunate to benefit from the
loyal service of Flt Lt Harvey Pole (R.G.C. 1952–56) on the
officer strength. His role in the development of the section until
his retirement was invaluable. Many members of the teaching
staff have been involved, including Margaret Houlihan, who
commanded and developed the section for a number of years,
Scott McKenzie, Neil Johnson, Mark McCrum, Roy Wakeford
and Duncan Carnegie.

Local camps at R.A.F. Buchan and R.A.F. Lossiemouth have
been excellent. At Buchan we were told the story (allegedly
true) of the lady living in a neighbouring property who wrote
to the Ministry of Defence expressing her concern over the
deplorable conditions under which servicemen and women
were working. Dozens were seen to enter a small Buchan farm-
house each day, emerging only after a long shift. She was unaware
that only the shell of the building remained (adjacent to the
well-known "golf ball" on the side of the Boddam hillside) and
that underneath was one of the largest underground bunkers
in the UK, housing the radar screens and early-warning systems
which had protected the country from the threat from the East
throughout the Cold War.

Lossiemouth, the UK's largest fast jet base, is another historic
airfield from which Lancaster bombers of 617 (Dambusters)
Sqn launched their final and decisive attack on the *Tirpitz* in

Tromso Fjord on 12th November 1944. Activities during two Lossiemouth camps have included visits to 617 Sqn (now based permanently at R.A.F. Lossiemouth), and XV Sqn both operating the Tornado GR4 aircraft.

Undoubtedly the highlight of the 2006 R.A.F. Valley camp was the opportunity for each and every one for the cadets to "fly" the BAE Systems Hawk Synthetic Training Facility (H.S.T.F.), the advanced jet training aircraft simulator used for fast jet pilot training. This is one of the most advanced simulators worldwide, and provided a fascinating experience for the cadets, whether performing aerobatics over the airfield or low flying through the Welsh mountains before landing the aircraft back at R.A.F. Valley. Cadets were thrilled when the entire 2006 Red Arrows team trained on the simulator in the morning and then left us to make the most of it in the afternoon, with one of their former members as our instructor! The author enjoyed being flown over Snowdon (at several hundred knots, inverted) by Cadet Mhairi McGregor, and one member of staff (not R.G.C.) was sick merely standing on the sidelines watching!

The section has also visited museums in Manchester and at East Fortune, the Battle of Britain Bunker at R.A.F. Uxbridge, the Cabinet War Rooms, the R.A.F. museums at Hendon and Cosford and the Imperial War Museums in London and at Duxford. A highlight for the section is the annual September outing to the Air Show at R.A.F. Leuchars.

Many individual cadets have benefited from participation in the prestigious annual national Air Cadet Leadership Course (the R.A.F. equivalent of the Army's Frimley Park course for the top 150 out of 40,000 Air Cadets annually). The author has been involved in this activity for twelve years and it is a matter of some pride that no fewer than three R.G.C. C.C.F. officers, Sqn Ldr Montgomery, Flt Lt Neil Johnson and F.O. Duncan Carnegie, were invited to act as flight commanders on the Directing Staff at R.A.F. College Cranwell in 2007. Given that there are some 2,000 potential volunteers for these positions and only thirty who are selected, this is a clear indication that leadership training offered at R.G.C. is of the highest standard.

Other cadets have been awarded Flying Scholarships or Gliding Scholarships. Early recipients included Flt Sgt Nick Smalley and Sgt Gerald Wyatt and more recently C.W.O. Thomas Hansford and C.W.O. Tim Thornton. One senior cadet, Sgt Ross Cameron, completed the Pilot Navigation course, which included the services of a pilot and use of a Hawk advanced jet training aircraft for five hours of navigation training over wide areas of England.

Some cadets are more adventurous than others. Flt Sgt Andrew Christie, Sgt Claire Hopkins, Sgt Ben Hewson and Cpl Chris Smart undertook parachute training culminating in a jump at Strathallan Airfield. Staff in recent years have shown no inclination to repeat this experience although it remains a possibility for the future!

We have been delighted to have benefited from tremendous support from Gordonian Flt Lt Greg House (R.G.C. 1982–88). He has taken a keen interest in the progress of cadets through the section, bringing aircraft including a Tucano and a Tornado to Dyce on several occasions to provide fascinating visits for the cadets. He also finds time to address the cadets and parents during his visits, and has been an invaluable source of information to potential applicants to the R.A.F. Greg has served in a variety of roles including flying the Tornado F3 at R.A.F. Leuchars where he hosted visits by our R.A.F. Section cadets. He is currently Sqn Q.F.I. with XXV(F) Sqn. at R.A.F. Leeming flying the Tornado F3 aircraft. He has recently been involved in the interception of 2 Russian Tu-160 Blackjack supersonic strategic bombers approaching British airspace during a period of renewed activity by the Russian Air Force. He left for the Falklands in February 2008 for his final tour there flying the Tornado before returning to R.A.F. Leeming to participate in activities connected with the disbanding of XXV Sqn. Greg will finish his career with the R.A.F. as an instructor on the Tutor aircraft instructing University Air Squadron students before joining a civilian company in autumn 2008. Greg, former Headmaster George Allan and Assistant Head Rona Livingstone (whose Gordonian son Duncan is a former Lord Lieutenant's Cadet and is an officer in the R.A.F.) have all given very generous donations of trophies which are awarded to top R.A.F. cadets on an annual basis. Greg's trophy is for the Most Promising Recruit in S2 and it has been highly pleasing to note the progress in subsequent years of recipients including Thomas Hansford and Tim Thornton.

The section has had considerable success since its formation only fourteen years ago, as can be seen in a later section of this work. In addition to the staff, the role played by founding and early members in establishing the strong reputation of the section has been crucial. Thanks are due (with apologies to the many prominent young people not named here) to cadets including Michelle Cope, Christian Arno, Roddy Powolny, Greig Nicol, Katrina Hepburn, Martin Stannard, Alistair Price, Lois Thomson, Peter Christie, Dara Richards, Lauren Ewen-MacMillan, Stephanie Lawson and Craig Kelly.

Chapter Eleven

THE PIPE BAND

The minute of the meeting of the Secondary School Committee of 11th December 1914 tells of contributions from staff and others towards the purchase of instruments for a "drum and fife band" to operate within the Cadet Corps. Music had of course featured strongly in the life of the school much earlier than this as witnessed by the magnificent Hospital Drum displayed in the Governors' Room. This drum, purchased in 1835, was played at a number of official functions across the city including the openings of Duthie Park, the Victoria Dock and the New Market. The success of the 1914 venture is not known, and it is some time before records indicate piping on a larger scale in the College. In the Gordonian of December 1941 it is recorded that there was enthusiasm but that "one side drum, four chanters and four sets pipes" were required. It was also noted that "the gift of these, loan or opportunity to buy would be greatly appreciated" (p.213). Originally, instruments were bought with donations from the Former Pupils' Association with additional funds being raised through a whist drive and popular dances in the MacRobert Hall to fight the "ever increasing financial problem" of supplying instruments and uniform. It is understood that initiatives over the years from the pupils themselves through which it was hoped to raise money were many and various, with some more successful than others!

Headmaster David Collier M.C. (described as a tall, lean man in a three-piece suit and Homburg hat, starched white collar and, on occasion, spats) was approached by Murdo McRae who asked for permission to start the band. This was granted, on condition that there was no cost to the school. The December 1947 *Gordonian* mentions a "very handsome donation from The Gordonians" along with additional funds coming from the General Purposes Fund and the A.C.F. Welfare Fund which would allow the formation of a "College Cadet Company's Pipe Band":

> Already we have a number of enthusiastic cadets waiting for the word "Go!". We are fortunate indeed that some of them are already proficient in the arts of "blowing" and "beating". The remainder are keen to learn ... There must be, we think, in the homes of Gordonians, some pipe band equipment which has ceased to be of use to its present owner, but which would be of great value to us ... Gifts should be sent to the O.C. Cadet Company, Robert Gordon's College. (p.209)

It was reported in the *Gordonian* of June 1948 that, following a period of preparation, the Pipe Band, under Murdo McRae, was now "fully operational". Only one piper had any previous experience, but from the outset, the C.C.F. Pipe Band gained a strong reputation. The first instructor was Pipe Major Cherry Anderson, Gordon Highlanders. The father of founding member Walter Anderson, he had led 51 Brigade into Tripoli only five years earlier, in January 1943. Former members stress the important role of John Runcie, who, starting at the tender age of thirteen, performed the remarkable feat of training a drum corps from scratch. John's recollections make interesting reading:

> The band started and we drummers met in Dr Forrest's room where we were introduced to an Army drumming instructor. As I was a reasonably proficient drummer through my dance band experience I sat out when the drummer started his instruction of the roll. Noticing me sitting out he then asked me to demonstrate, which I did unfortunately somewhat better than him. He never came back and I was lumbered with teaching

the drummers during my remaining five years at school. We moved to the room of Mr Broadley, the Principal Teacher of Geography, where we played on his table and dimpled the surface, which he never complained about. After five years the band started playing at all school events including Founder's Day and Sports Day. We also initiated the tradition of the band playing at the end of the school year when those leaving performed a gigantic reel. Many leavers have mentioned this as a perfect ending to their time at the school. A regular engagement was playing at the University Charities Parade and leading all the other bands which participated.

Besides teaching drumming, my other function was helping acquire as many items as possible for the band. I discovered a Charlie Smith, who had innumerable connections, and had access to a large supply of ex-Army kilts and service dress, which he let us have at very low cost. He also helped us acquire side drums. We also made good use of all the second-hand shops in the city. I remember a Mr Blackhall, a dealer in Marischal Street, who was very helpful in giving us goods at what I am sure was less than cost price. I remember going on several occasions with Mr McLaughlan, who I think was O.C. of the cadets at the time. He had the cash, but I did the bargaining. The most difficult thing to acquire was bass and tenor drummers' tiger skins, which were necessary adornments at the time. These skins were a great attraction to children within and outside the school, who were keen to feel the sharp teeth in the tigers' heads. General O'Connor of North African Campaign fame inspected the unit. He was impressed by the band and offered to donate a pipe banner. Being an Art pupil I was asked to arrange this, and the banner was designed by Mr Burnett of the Art Department. The banner duly arrived from Isac Benzies along with a second banner from General O'Connor. Following a misunderstanding, we now had two banners, only one of which the general had agreed to fund. I decided to run a Raffle amongst the drummers and the banner was paid for. The band by this time had two rooms. We used the armoury as the armourer, Ian "Pop" Macauley, was our big drummer. We used to tension our drums by pulling the drum ropes, which was a strenuous exercise. The other room was at the top of the Auld Hoose and was where we kept our band clothing and kitted out new members.

I remember that during camp at Barry Buddon there was a NAAFI but also a large YMCA or Salvation Army structure which was much cheaper and where we would all congregate. We had the battle of the bands, when one school band would approach another, both playing, and attempt to put the other out of step and time. We had an amazingly loud beat from our big drum and were always victorious. Our pipe tutor, Fergie, would also get our marching up to scratch by making us parade and play on the sand at the beach.

The next camp was at Gairelochead. We visited the battle-ship *King George* V, which was moored nearby. All wanted to go to the highest crow's nest. Fergie also attempted to teach us all highland dancing and at one point we were visited by the Headmaster. You could see the consternation on our faces with the Head and the O.C. approaching as they heard Fergie shouting "To Hell, to Hell!". The mood lightened when they discovered he was only giving the dance instruction "Toe, heel . . . toe, heel".

The band visited London for the Festival of Britain in 1948, and in the same year, two pipers represented the College at the Youth Festival in Paris. In 1949 the band led the school to church on Founder's Day for the first time, in a tradition which exists to this day. Later in the year four pipers and one drummer (John Runcie) were selected to play in a massed North-East Cadet Forces Pipe Band in the presence of Winston Churchill and Field Marshal Montgomery at the El Alamein Annual

Reunion at Earls Court, London. In April 1950 the band was invited to lead the Aberdeen University Torchlight Procession. In 1953 the band played at a match between North District and the All Blacks, and band members joined the Aberdeen University O.T.C. band to play at the Coronation Parade. Members also recall a wide range of events including a march from Bridge of Don to Blackdog (taking turns to play) and one occasion when Douglas Bennett, an extremely smart Drum Major, suffered a failure of elastic in an item of clothing whilst marking time outside the church on Founder's Day. Band members enjoyed the military training at Summer Camp along with the opportunity to extend their piping experience.

In the 1950s and '60s there was tremendous mutual support between R.G.C. and Aberdeen University O.T.C. bands, with the O.T.C. relying heavily on R.G.C. (and Aberdeen Grammar School) for their success. Four College Band pipe majors were fully committed to Aberdeen University O.T.C. Pipe Band whilst still R.G.C. pupils – Kenny Melvin, Walter Anderson, Graham (Kiki) Whyte and Bill Fraser. All led the band to success in the inter-university O.T.C. band competition (and it is noted that the O.T.C. band had not enjoyed success before the involvement of our pupils!). Ex-R.G.C. drummers formed most of the drum corps in the O.T.C. band. Younger players extended their experience playing in the O.T.C. band at, for example, the Torchlight Procession while "old boys" frequently returned to play for the College at events such as Founder's Day, the annual highlight.

Early members of the band went on to enjoy a lifetime of involvement in piping. Norman Matheson edited the Brown and Nicoll tapes and has been involved in judging at Braemar. Walter Anderson is well known in piping in Burntisland and South Fife, while Alex Urquhart became World Champion Drum Major and provided highly valued drumming tuition at the College. Alex's son Ramsay was later Pipe Major (1980–83), and Alex has continued to take a keen interest in the Band and the C.C.F. over the years. Bill Fraser, who is well known in piping circles, returned to the College as a piping instructor for a lengthy period in the late 1960s and '70s. Frequent mention is made of him in the *Gordonian* magazines of the time, thanking him and Drum Sgt Colin Rae for their assistance.

A strong tradition of annual performances at local hospitals and old folks' homes developed in the 1970s, along with appearances at events such as Junior and Senior Sports Days, the Sillerton House coffee morning, performances at Haddo House, Methlick, and the St Margaret's School Sports Day. 1972 was a year of some importance with the additional incentive to potential pipers that the bagpipes were now to be considered an "acceptable instrument" for those boys taking the S.C.E. course in Music.

Jim Hamilton joined the staff of the College History Department in 1974 and began the first of two periods of involvement with the band. He recalls that all 1974 band members, Robert and Hector Sutherland, Gavin Downie, David Williamson, Ian and David Walker and Ronvald Garden, had been tutored by Bill Fraser. Pipe majors during this period were Robert and Hector Sutherland with Leading Drummers Philip Pratt and Andrew Milne. Dress at this time was traditional, consisting of green tunics, crossbelt/waistbelt, military hairy sporran, spats and diced hose. Only spats for adults were provided, however, and proved something of a challenge to fit to the legs of a twelve year old!

Several families made outstanding contributions to the success of the band. No fewer than five members of the Sutherland family were involved: brothers Robert and Hector as pipe majors, Simon as bass drummer and their cousins Andrew and James as pipers. David Smylie was said to have put his "life and soul" into all aspects of his school life with the Pipe Band being no exception. He approached Jim in the playground during rehearsal one day to enquire about membership. On being told that three years of practice would be needed in order to reach the required standard, he promised to be ready in one. Evidence of his success was his appointment as pipe major within the three-year period already mentioned. David, who works as a doctor in New Zealand, still plays and has regular contact with Jim.

Jim returned to the College as clerk of works and band tutor between 1989 and 1994 and enjoyed a highly successful period with pipe majors such as Thorvald Garden and Michael and Paul Ritchie along with leading drummers Colin Cumming and Philip Booth. The band had been through a difficult period and Jim, with his "passion and dedication" was central in "resurrecting the band from a sorry state" during which it had been "tutor-less and wandering" according to *Gordonian* magazines of 1989 and '90. New drums were purchased "not before time" (and thanks expressed to the Parents Association). Many pupils were keen to learn. The band paraded in the 1993–94 session with eighteen pipers and some eight drummers who were tutored by Mrs L. Greenwell. A further innovation was the appointment of a drum major (tutored by Alex Urquhart) who led the band on Founder's Day 1994. The band also competed successfully on two occasions, at Glenalmond and in Edinburgh, in the annual Independent Schools' Championship. Michael and Paul Ritchie were enthusiastic participants who were always willing to pass on their expertise and assist in the instruction of learners. A highlight of this period in the history of the band was the performance given during the visit of H.R.H. The Princess Royal for the official opening of Countesswells. This was not the first occasion on which former Cameron Highlander Jim Hamilton had been involved in piping for the Princess, having worked as a piper on H.M.Y. *Britannia* in 1958 following service in Aden and Korea. Jim's son James was also a band member during his time at the College in the late 1970s. Granddaughter Emma Hamilton was a senior Army Section cadet who completed the Cadet Leadership Course in 2007.

Other members of staff thanked in the *Gordonian* over the

years included John Jermieson and Charles Morton (administration), Mrs L. Bain, Mrs D. Brow and Mr Robert Sutherland for their "invaluable tuition".

Many notable Gordonians were associated with piping while at the College, including former Scottish Liberal Democrat Leader and former Deputy First Minister Nicol Stephen M.S.P. (side drummer) and Chairman of the Governors Colin Crosby (bass drummer).

Lindsay Gilchrist, in whose name the prize for the Best All Rounder in S2 was donated, was a keen and promising chanter player at the time of his tragic road accident.

The young age and enthusiasm of the present-day musicians is extremely encouraging. In addition to collective piping there is a strong tradition of participation in individual competition. Former Pipe Major Paul Ritchie has had particular success in solo piping, notably a win in "B" Grade light music at the Northern Meeting. In recent times he has played with the Shotts & Dykes band. There has been particular success in recent years by Pipe Majors Thomas Fraser (R.G.C. 1989–2001 and son of Dr Bill Fraser) and Fraser Maitland (R.G.C. 1993–2006). Whilst at the College, Thomas won a McGregor Medal at Oban, the Junior Pibroch at Northern Meetings twice and the Scottish Schools Pibroch Championship in four consecutive years. Fraser Maitland, who now plays with Aberdeen University Officers' Training Corps Drums and Pipes, displays considerable ability. Awards whilst still at school included C.C.F. Senior Piping Champion, Runner-up Under-eighteen Northern Meeting, 3rd MacGregor Memorial & Under-18 Champion Piper at Aberdeen & Braemar Highland Games 2006–07. Former Pipe Major Ian Christie is also competing successfully around the Highland Games. The band is fortunate to have had players of this calibre. It is always a particular pleasure to see the enthusiasm shown by very young musicians from the Junior School and early stages of the Senior School who will be with us for some time to come.

Piping continues to enjoy considerable success today in the very capable hands of Jim Hamilton's successor, Captain Mike Maitland, who also serves as a C.C.F. Army Section officer. Mike joined the College staff in 1993 following twenty-two years of regular service in the R.A.F. and is an experienced piper in his own right. Mike's first year in the post saw many performances at events such as the College Burns Supper, the U.K. Under-sixteen Basketball competition and the International Professional Women's Charity Organisation event in the Beach Ballroom by pipers such as Nikki Wottge, Craig Guyan, Chris Levings and Jane Riddell. Mike and sons Fraser and Lewis continue the family tradition of commitment to piping in the College of the Sutherland, Hamilton, Urquhart and Fraser and other families. We have also been fortunate to gain the services of Gordonian and former band leading drummer Eileen Mutch who conducts drumming instruction. Various public performances, notably Founder's Day, Sports Day and at Crathes Castle, do much to encourage piping amongst younger pupils and also to promote the College in the city and beyond.

Founding and past members have been generous in their support of the present-day band. Alex Urquhart donated a magnificent Drum Major's mace in September 2000 along with a very fine trophy for the C.C.F. cadet showing the greatest "initiative" over the course of a year. More recently, at a reunion in 2007 to mark the 60th anniversary of the founding of the band, a pipe banner was presented to Pipe Major Ian Christie by founding and former members.

It is a source of great pride that at the time of the re-badging of Army units to the Highlanders and more recently the Royal Regiment of Scotland, the decision was taken to retain the Gordon Highlanders badge for our Pipe Band. Contrary to popular belief the badge is consequently still in use, and we are, to the best of our knowledge, the last remaining unit to wear the badge associated with the great traditions of the local regiment.

Chapter Twelve

ACHIEVEMENTS AND AWARDS

Over the years, our C.C.F. teams and individuals have been highly successful at local and national level. The degree of success enjoyed has been quite out of proportion to the numbers of cadets involved and reflects the very high quality and degree of commitment of our young people.

Lord Lieutenant's Cadets

In recent years we have been delighted that several cadets have been appointed Lord Lieutenant's Cadet. This is a highly prestigious appointment, with the recipient accompanying the Lord Lieutenant at numerous official functions representing H.M. The Queen in the city of Aberdeen. These appointments, each for a period of twelve months, have heightened the profile of the College in the city, and have been a fitting reward for the commitment and achievements of the cadets concerned.

Neil Cargill, Lord Lieutenant's Cadet 1998 (and later Senior Under-Officer, Aberdeen University O.T.C.), began training at the Royal Military Academy Sandhurst in May 2004 before commissioning into The Highlanders. He then served as platoon commander of 6 Platoon, B Company, The Highlanders, 4th Battalion, The Royal Regiment of Scotland. Having served in Iraq in 2006, he began 2007 in France leading his Battalion's team in the Biathlon Competiton and is currently at Catterick training recruits at the Infantry Training Centre. Captain Cargill hopes to organize a visit by some of our senior cadets to The Highlanders base in Germany in the future.

R.A.F. Section Sgt **Isabel Wreford** had a highly successful year in 2002–03 (including undertaking a wind-surfing course with the Royal Navy) before departing to study at Oxford, through which she has undertaken work for her Geology course in Greece and Chile.

Cadet Warrant Officer **Thomas Hansford** (see below) was appointed Lord Lieutenant's Cadet 2004–05. He was presented to H.R.H. The Prince of Wales and the Duchess of Cornwall (on her very first official engagement) at the Gordon Highlanders Museum during his year as Lord Lieutenant's Cadet.

During 2005–2006, Colour Sergeant **Fraser Maitland** had a highly successful and enjoyable year. **Sarah Beaton** was also involved in a number of engagements during her appointment in 2006–07, and was presented to H.R.H. The Princess Royal in November 2006.

June 2007 saw the appointment of another Lord Lieutenant's Cadet, Sgt **Timothy Thornton** (also mentioned below) and he is making the most of his time in the post. The appointment of Colour Sergeant **Christopher Gray** of the Army Section has been confirmed for 2008–09 and he is looking forward to the opportunities this will bring. We are extremely grateful to the Reserve Forces and Cadets Association and the successive Lords Lieutenant who have provided these young people with such fascinating and memorable experiences.

National Awards

Recipients of highly prestigious awards in recent years have been Cadet Warrant Officer **Thomas Hansford**, Sgt **Liam McNeil**, and Flt Sgt **Timothy Thornton**. Thomas was awarded a Sixth Form Scholarship and was the only C.C.F. cadet from Scotland to be awarded a place on the prestigious 2005 International Air Cadet Exchange. He featured strongly in the Young Aberdonian of the Year competition, but his main achievement was being named the top UK C.C.F. (R.A.F.) cadet of 2005. He was presented with the Sir John Thomson Memorial Sword by Lady Thomson during Air Squadron Day at R.A.F. Cranwell. This event was attended by Mrs Denise Hansford (Thomas's mother), Head of College Hugh Ouston, Sqn Ldr Montgomery, Flt Lt Neil Johnson and Flt Lt Greg House, and was one of the most impressive days in the history of our C.C.F. unit. Thomas led the parade at which the R.A.F. Band played and, following the awards ceremony, all guests enjoyed what was in effect a private air display, Thomas experiencing a lengthy flight in a Tiger Moth aircraft while Mr Ouston was flown in a Piper Cub aircraft by former BA Concorde pilot Captain John Hutchinson. Thomas was then driven to R.A.F. Linton-on-Ouse by Flt Lt House, where he flew the Tucano aircraft. At the time, no fewer than four Gordonians, Lt Cdr Pete Lumsden and Flt Lts House, Anton Wisely and Tim Clement were working as Qualified Flying Instructors on the base. Thomas was later awarded the John Cunningham Trophy (named after Group Captain John "Cat's Eyes" Cunningham C.B.E., D.S.O. and two Bars, D.F.C. and Bar, the most famous R.A.F. night fighter pilot of the Second World War) for an outstanding performance during his Flying Scholarship, again being rated top in the UK. He is currently reading Physics at Christ Church, Oxford, sponsored by the R.A.F.

Like Thomas Hansford, Flt Sgt **Timothy Thornton** was the recipient of the Flt Lt Greg House Award as Best R.A.F. Section Recruit during his S2 year (2004). A current Lord Lieutenant's Cadet, he has now been awarded a place on the International Air Cadet Exchange 2008 (when he will travel to Israel), a Commandant Air Cadets' Certificate for Outstanding Service to the C.C.F., a Gliding Scholarship, a Flying Scholarship and an R.A.F. Sixth Form Scholarship. Nominated by us for the Sir John Thomson Memorial Sword, he was placed in the top six UK C.C.F. R.A.F. cadets and was presented with a Geoffrey de

Havilland Medal during Air Squadron Day at R.A.F. Cranwell in June 2008. He hopes to study Aeronautical Engineering at either Southampton or Worcester College, Oxford, before entering the R.A.F. for flying training.

Cadet Leadership Courses

Leadership training is one of the fundamental aims of the C.C.F. and is experience which may be of considerable use to cadets in promoted positions within the C.C.F., positions of responsibility in the school and in their future lives and careers. It is highly desirable that cadets, particularly those aspiring to senior positions within the C.C.F., undertake one of the three prestigious national courses, the Cadet Leadership course at Frimley Park or Nesscliff, Shropshire, or the Air Cadet Leadership Course at the R.A.F. College, Cranwell.

These strenuous weeks provide a mix of theoretical and practical activities, placing participants in charge of their team in increasingly challenging situations as the week progresses. Students gain an insight into the training provided at the Royal Military Academy, Sandhurst, and the R.A.F. College, Cranwell, should they later consider a military career, but the leadership training is designed to be general in nature. Courses run at Easter and in July and cater for the very top UK Army Cadet Force, Air Training Corps and C.C.F. cadets. These courses are widely acknowledged to be the very best of all the activities offered by the cadet organizations. The number of R.G.C. cadets attending courses is high and cadets can be proud of their achievements. Easter 2008 saw five cadets of the Army Section successfully completing the course at Nesscliff: Angus Coull, Chris Gray, Ross MacFarlan, Tamzyn Mathers and Thomas Rust. Thomas and Chris also overcame very stiff opposition to be awarded well-deserved Army Scholarships in April 2008 and hope to pursue careers in the Army.

Liam McNeil was awarded a last-minute place on the Air Cadet Leadership Course at R.A.F. Cranwell in July 2007. This course is the only activity open to both Air Training Corps and C.C.F. (R.A.F. Section) cadets. It is an arduous course and standards are extremely high, with only the very best 160 Air Cadets from a membership of 42,000 completing the course each summer. Liam did extremely well to complete the course and to be named Best Cadet of his week, particularly given his young age of sixteen years one month at the time of the course (the minimum age being sixteen). Liam led the passing-out parade in front of the R.A.F. College building on the Saturday morning. Some weeks later, he was informed that he had been named overall Best Cadet of the 2007 courses and was to be awarded the Cubby Sword in recognition of this outstanding achievement. The impressive presentation, by Wing Commander George Clayton-Jones of H.Q. Air Cadets, R.A.F. Cranwell, took place in the Governors' Room on 2nd November 2007.

Following Thomas Hansford's award, Liam's success means that individuals from our R.A.F. Section have received the two top UK Air Cadet awards within a period of two years.

Not to be outdone, Cpl Innes Worsman of the Army Section was given an award for being in the "Best Section" during his July 2007 Cadet Leadership Course at the Cadet Training Centre, Frimley Park. He also won a Gold medal for his performance as Best Cadet in the orienteering and assault course elements of the week. It is highly pleasing to have had both an R.A.F. and an Army Section cadet receive these awards in the same year, given the strong competition from outstanding young people from all over the UK.

The Scottish C.C.F. Military Skills Competition

This is a particularly demanding competition involving a weekend of constant activity in which teams are tested in a wide variety of areas. Elements of the competition include First Aid, mounting a patrol, a section attack, shooting, map reading and an obstacle course. Of particular note is the fact that the team leader is expected to lead his team throughout the weekend; staff involvement is minimal and the leader has the responsibility of ensuring the welfare of the team members (including all domestic arrangements), timekeeping and preparation for the different events. The Army Section gained first place in the Scottish C.C.F. Military Skills Competition in October 2004 during a tough but thoroughly enjoyable weekend culminating in a flight for all members of the winning team in a Gazelle helicopter as a reward for their success. Although failing to win in subsequent years, the Army Section can nevertheless be extremely proud to have come second in Scotland in 2005, third in 2006 and second in 2007.

The National C.C.F. (R.A.F.) Ground Training Competition

The R.A.F. Section has had considerable success in national competitions, winning through on many occasions to represent the "Scotnine" area of Scotland, Northern Ireland and the North of England in the final of the National Ground Training Competition at R.A.F. Uxbridge, London. This tough competition involves drill, turnout, fitness, shooting, command tasks, teamwork, aircraft recognition and First Aid. As Scottish Champions in 2007 we once again competed in the UK final and were delighted to be placed second in the First Aid element of the competition and seventh overall out of 186 schools. Although not participating in the London final of the 2005 competition, due only to changes in the regulations governing geographical areas, the section was placed first in Scotland in four out of five years during this highly successful period.

2004 was a particularly pleasing year for our C.C.F. teams, with both the R.A.F. and Army sections featuring as "Scottish champions" in their respective national competitions.

The Aberdeen Wapinschaw

Between the Army and R.A.F. sections, no fewer than five Wapinschaw trophies were won in 2006, seven in 2007 and five in 2008. Success has not been limited to team competitions, with Cpl Kirsty Sneddon in 2007 and L. Cpl Thomas Murdoch in 2008 recording the highest individual scores of the day and being awarded the Individual Trophy. The Wapinschaw or "weapons show" has its origins as far back as 1424 when, under James I, the parliament, sitting at Perth, passed the Act which read:

> It is ordanyt in ilk scherifdome of ye realme ther be maid Wapynschawing four tymis I' ye zer.

Citizens were encouraged to meet and demonstrate that they not only possessed weapons, but were able to show a reasonable level of skill in using them, should they be required to undertake military service.

Parliament later passed another act which described the procedure to be followed at these meetings, the persons by whom they were to be conducted and the penalties that would result from failure to obey. From then on, and for more than 300 years, there are numerous enactments in the statute book and the proceedings of the Privy Council of Scotland relating to "Wapinshawingis" and preparedness to defend the realm.

In Aberdeen, the earliest reference to such a gathering in the minutes of the Town Council occurs in 1496 when the burgesses were required:

> to compeir personalie one Monunday the XVIII day of July instant at the Cunnegar Hil.

The establishment of the National Rifle Association, which held annual competitions in England, led to the development of the Aberdeen Wapinschaw into a three-day meeting in July

1862 with competitions for rifles, carbines and artillery, with 68-pounder guns firing at targets floating almost a mile out in Aberdeen Bay.

In 1869 Queen Victoria presented the first of the prizes which she gave annually throughout her lifetime. Thereafter King Edward VII continued the practice and King George V presented a challenge cup which is the Blue Riband of the individual rifle competition today. This generous encouragement has been of inestimable value to the Wapinschaw and the present Association is very proud that Her Majesty Queen Elizabeth II is its patron.

With the exception of the years of the First and Second World Wars, the Wapinschaw has been held annually since 1862. Throughout, the Association has attempted to keep the competitions reasonably in line with current shooting practices whilst at the same time trying to maintain the traditional atmosphere of the meeting.

In more recent years the Wapinschaw has been financially supported by the Highland Territorial and Auxiliary Volunteer Reserve Association (T.A.V.R.A.) and the Reserve Forces and Cadets Association (R.F.C.A.). In 1996, Highland R.F.C.A. took over the running of the event. The Wapinschaw Committee is drawn from R.F.C.A., tri-service Reserve Forces and Cadets Personnel and civilian gun clubs.

In 2004, 51st (Scottish) Brigade became the sponsor of the Wapinschaw, supplying manpower, materials and infrastructure.

A unique collection of magnificent trophies is now offered annually for team and individual competitions. Our Acting Honorary Colonel, R.F.C.A. former Chairman Lt Col A. R. Cram T.D., is President of the Wapinschaw Association.

Best Cadet at R.A.F. Camp

R.A.F. Section camps differ from Army camps in that cadets live and work closely throughout the week of camp in mixed flights with cadets from many leading UK independent schools. It has been highly gratifying that on many occasions our young people have stood out from cadets from these other schools to feature consistently as "Best Cadet" of the week. The reward for one such recipient, Sgt Ross Cameron, was a flight in the Battle of Britain Memorial Flight Lancaster bomber. This was a unique occasion and certainly a story for the grandchildren of the cadet involved! Another cadet, Nicholas Gordon, was only denied a Hawk flight following his nomination as Best Cadet at R.A.F. Valley in 2006 as he had not reached the minimum weight needed for the safe operation of the ejector seat and parachute in an emergency. This was particularly disappointing, although an additional hour-long session in the Hawk simulator with one of the country's top instructors was something of a consolation.

Chapter Thirteen

A GENERAL EDUCATION

Leadership

On meeting our senior cadets, visitors and those with whom we have contact at events outwith the College invariably speak of their impression of confident, articulate and enthusiastic young men and women who are developing into future leaders and highly effective contributors to society. On many occasions we have heard the phrase "a fine ambassador for the College".

It is fully acknowledged that only a few of our R.G.C. cadets are likely to embark upon military careers, and training reflects the need for leadership skills in all areas of civilian life. 21 Cadet Training Team assist College staff on a weekly basis and do much to encourage leadership skills amongst Army Section cadets. They offer, for example, lectures and practical experience in instructional techniques. In their senior years, cadets are expected to plan, organise and deliver much of the instruction to younger cadets. The Methods of Instruction or "Teacher Training" course delivered by 21 C.T.T. is impressive, as is the performance of our senior cadets who respond well to instruction and learn quickly to deliver effective lessons in a highly competent and confident manner.

The Royal Air Force Section offers its own training, based on the Air Cadet Leadership Course. It is particularly important that all cadets undertake this training as they approach their senior years. Promotion to senior ranks depends on this having been completed, and leadership training is one of the three requirements of the Advanced award in the R.A.F. Proficiency Syllabus, which the majority of cadets should aim to complete before the end of S6. Cadets are required to attend lectures which are devised by us and which reflect training in the theory of leadership taught not only on the Air Cadet Leadership Course but also to officer cadets at the R.A.F. College, Cranwell. Various styles of and approaches to leadership are discussed, and cadets are introduced to the "Functional Leadership" techniques as practised throughout the Royal Air Force.

Training days for both sections are organised, frequently at Countesswells or Gordon Barracks, Bridge of Don. Cadets put theory into practice in a series of leadership tasks designed to put a leader under pressure and show him/her how he/she performs when in command of a team of subordinates in situations which become increasingly complex. Cadets must take it in turn to lead and to act as team members. Responsibilities also ensure that cadets are kept under pressure at all times, even when not in the lead, as "teamwork" is stressed, not simply leadership.

In order to complete training, cadets must satisfy staff that they have, for an appropriate period of time, held a position of responsibility and gained experience of leading. This is similar to training in the "Skill" area for the Duke of Edinburgh's Award Scheme. Appropriate experience to be undertaken is agreed between staff and the cadet, and, where possible, reflects other roles which may be held by a cadet. These might include College Prefect, House Captain, Team Captain, Scout/Guide Leader, appropriate voluntary work out of school or many other posts requiring initiative and leadership skills.

Former Pupils

Over the years, many former pupils and cadets have indeed embarked upon successful military careers. Only a few are listed here and apologies are offered to the very many additional distinguished former pupils who do not feature.

Former Pupil **Major-General John T. Coull** C.B., F.R.C.S., F.R.C.S.E. (R.G.C. 1939–52) held various posts including Medico-Legal Advisor, Army Medical Directorate, M.o.D., Director of Army Surgery and Col. Commandant, R.A.M.C. He gave the Founder's Day Oration in 2004. **Col. Roland Buchan** T.D. (R.G.C. 1950–54) completed National Service before serving in a variety of Territorial roles. He commanded G. Company, Gordon Highlanders, formed after the amalgamation of all Gordons Territorial units, before serving for three tours as Cadet Commandant, 14 Battalion Gordon Highlanders (Army Cadet Force) which covered Aberdeenshire, Banffshire, Kincardineshire and Aberdeen City. He retains a keen interest in the C.C.F. of today. **Col. Alistair Flett** (R.G.C. 1949–55) held various posts in R.E.M.E. through the Territorial Army and became Honorary Colonel of R.E.M.E. (Scotland). He is well known to the College through his academic work as a university lecturer in Physics.

Others from this period included two senior R.A.F. officers. **Jim Rennie** (R.G.C. 1953–59) returned to the College as a teacher of Mathematics after studying at the University of Aberdeen and Aberdeen College of Education. He later joined the Royal Air Force as an Education Officer, graduating from the Royal Air Force College, Cranwell with the Sword of Honour as Best Overall Cadet of his course. He held many posts including Officer Commanding, Airmen's Command School, R.A.F. Hereford and Station Commander, R.A.F. Innsworth. He studied at the National Defence College and worked on Training Development Policy for the Ministry of Defence, reaching the rank of group captain. A keen sportsman, he contributed widely to rugby in the R.A.F. and holds the position of Life Vice-President of the R.A.F. Rugby Union. **Ian Junor**, as the recipient of a Royal Air Force Scholarship, was expected to be committed to membership of a cadet organization during his years at school. There being no R.A.F. Section of the College C.C.F., he became a member of 620 Sqn, Air Training Corps, based at Fairfield House on Whinhill Road (well known to many as the headquarters of Aberdeen University Air Squadron before the move of the squadron to R.A.F. Leuchars). He left the College in 1959 to attend the Royal Air Force College, Cranwell. He later commanded 35 Sqn which flew the Vulcan aircraft, and subsequently held M.o.D. posts including Deputy Director, Personnel, Plans and Policy, retiring from the R.A.F. as a group captain.

From the 1970s, former "Bunker" and C.C.F. cadet **Duncan Milne** (R.G.C. 1966–1974) flew the Nimrod aircraft at R.A.F. Kinloss. Air Training Corps cadet **Eric Porter** (R.G.C. 1969–1975), son of the late John Porter, a governor and great friend and supporter of the C.C.F., was another R.A.F. officer. Leading Drummer **Philip Pratt** (R.G.C. 1969–76) also joined the R.A.F. After leaving school, he was a member of Aberdeen University Air Squadron with Duncan, Eric and the author. Other former "Bunkers" C.S.M. **Kevin Harvey** and **Stuart Downie** (under John Dow in the 1980s) served in bomb disposal and in the US Armed Forces respectively. Also from this era, Commander **Craig Mearns** of the Logistics Branch of the Royal Navy is currently serving in Afghanistan. Two other former cadets have served as officers in the US Marines in Iraq. Others have served in Afghanistan. Maj. **Nick Champion** left R.G.C. in 1990 and is another former Army Section cadet. Major **Timothy Allan**, son of former Head George Allan, served in a number of roles including Equerry to H.R.H. The Duke of York. As previously stated, 1994–95 School Captain and Otaki Scholar **Anthony Liva** serves with the Royal Marines.

Wide Experience

With the varied career paths ahead of our cadets, training of a wide nature ensures the young people are knowledgeable about military matters as they leave the College. Care is taken, however, to ensure that all aspects of our training form part of the general education of our young people and provide experience which will be invaluable in later life.

It is interesting to read the editorial of the June 1919 *F.P. Association Magazine,* which reflects the main purpose of the C.C.F. as we see it in the twenty-first century. This is central to our aims and is reflected in our motto "In Learning is our Strength":

> In contemplating the new world, which was the hope of those who were sacrificed, we are more and more convinced that nothing counts as much as Education. (p. 4)

Staff and cadets were guests at Edinburgh Castle on 9th July 1999 on the occasion of the opening of the Scottish Parliament to witness parts of the procedures not open to the general public. Regular visits are made to the Gordon Highlanders Museum in Viewfield Road, with one senior cadet recently having undertaken work experience there throughout S6. Visiting speakers address the cadets on a wide range of subjects. Cadets have visited residents in the Erskine Hospital unit at Bridge of Don. It is hoped the C.C.F. may consider undertaking a charitable project on an annual basis in the near future.

Our annual Remembrance Service and Parade, attended by distinguished guests, has become an established tradition. Imaginative services have been led by our Honorary Padre, Rev. Dominic Smart, and by Rev. Lois Kinsey T.D. (both are parents of current or former C.C.F. cadets Meredith Smart and Louis and Harry Kinsey) and cadets speak of the event as meaningful and thought-provoking. This is one of the occasions in the year when the Army and R.A.F. Sections combine with members of the Pipe Band for a joint event, and the parade in front of the Auld Hoose is impressive. Senior cadets also join the School Captains and the President of the Gordonian Association at the annual College Remembrance Service and each lays a wreath at the War Memorial.

The location of the war grave of every Gordonian killed in the two World Wars has been researched by staff and senior cadets. Cemeteries in the North East and in Normandy have been visited and poppies are placed on the graves of some of our former pupils on the Friday closest to 11th November of each year. Cadets are reminded that casualties are not limited to wars in the first half of the last century. Most recently, the College community was saddened by the tragic training accident in 2006 which claimed the life of Lance Corporal Gordon Campbell, Royal Marines. Gordon was a pupil from 1991–97 and an enthusiastic and highly able Army Section cadet. He went on to serve in many theatres abroad and was praised in one particular commendation for "his personal contribution and exemplary performance under sustained pressure [which were] nothing short of outstanding" and his "calm, unfaltering efficiency and acceptance of responsibility [which] were remarkable".

The Duke of Edinburgh's Award Scheme has become a major part of the life of the College, with very large numbers of pupils (just under 400) participating in 2008. The scheme, dating from 1956, was first introduced to the College in 1963. The scheme was co-ordinated by John Gordon although hikes were organized by the C.C.F. The Air Training Corps is today the largest UK service provider for the scheme, and it is interesting to note similarities in the aims of training provided through cadet organizations and the D. of E. Scheme. Participation in, for example, C.C.F. leadership courses, can be counted as the residential element of the Duke of Edinburgh's Award at Gold level.

The following extracts are taken from the D. of E. Scheme website www.theaward.org:

It fosters self-discipline, enterprise and perseverance.

It is a programme of practical, cultural and adventurous activities designed for use by all agencies having a concern for the development of young people; a programme flexible enough to meet their enthusiasms and aptitudes whatever their background or culture, however plentiful or limited their resources may be.

In gaining Awards, young people learn by experience the importance of commitment, enterprise and effort. They discover a great deal about themselves and come to know the enjoyment of working with and for other people.

Through a commitment to its programmes, young people will be acquiring self-reliance and a sense of responsibility to others, both essential qualities of citizenship. The Award Programme is a vehicle for spiritual, personal and social development and the overall benefits of the Award are therefore greater than the sum of its component parts.

Introduced in 2003, the Edexcel BTEC First Diploma in Public Services is available to senior cadets and a few have completed the award. We also hope to participate in the M.V. Award scheme through which senior cadets can count time spent assisting with the supervision and teaching of younger cadets as voluntary service. Awards, which are endorsed by the Scottish Executive, are given for fifty, 100 and 200 hours of volunteering, with the 200 hours award signed by the First Minister.

Cadets are made aware of the strong links between the College and the MacRobert family. The College can claim no direct link with the MacRoberts in terms of military activity, but it would be wrong to continue without acknowledging the connection between the MacRobert and Gordon names. At an early age, Alexander MacRobert lectured at the Aberdeen Mechanics Institute and taught at Gordon's College evening classes. He soon departed for India, however, and followed a path which would see him as a Lieutenant Colonel in the Cawnpore Volunteers, knighted in 1910 for his humanitarian work, at the head of what would become the British India Corporation and created a Baronet in 1922.

After the death of his first wife, he married Rachel Workman, the daughter of well-known American Himalayan mountaineers, explorers and authors, despite an age difference of almost thirty years. They returned to the family home at Douneside, Tarland, with their three sons, Alasdair, Roderic and Iain. Despite the death of Sir Alexander in 1922, the family is described by AC Gunn in *The MacRobert Trusts 1943–1993* as highly prominent. The boys grew up reading of the exploits of Sir Malcolm Campbell, Amy Johnson and Charles Lindbergh. They enjoyed holidays on the family estate with "the noise of sports cars or motor cycles [which] broke the stillness in the tree-lined drive" (p.19). Tragically, the title was to pass from one brother to the next as one after the other was killed while flying. Sir Alasdair died in a flying accident in England shortly before the outbreak of the Second World War. He had founded an aviation company and was a "passionate devotee of flying". Flt Lt Sir Roderic died in Iraq whilst leading his Hurricane detachment on a raid on the airfield at Mosul. Pilot Officer Sir Iain died five weeks later flying with Costal Command whilst involved in the search for a downed bomber crew in the North Sea.

It was thought that Lady MacRobert would return home to America. Instead, she remained deeply involved in the life of the nation and local community. On the death of Sir Iain, her youngest son, she sent a cheque for £25,000 to the Secretary of State for War for the purchase of an aircraft in memory of her sons. The aircraft was to bear the name "MacRobert's Reply" and the family crest and, ideally, be piloted by a Scotsman. A Stirling bomber of XV Sqn was chosen. She would later purchase four Hurricane fighters for other squadrons. XV Sqn has ensured Lady MacRobert's gesture has been remembered to this day. The illustration in this work depicts a XV Sqn Tornado GR1 with tail number ZA587. During that year, the aircraft was used on several occasions by the Tornado GR1 display crew. Since then, aircraft have moved around and upgraded to GR4 standard and the current aircraft carrying the "MacRobert's Reply" crest is a Tornado GR4, ZA459.

Having shown tremendous generosity well before the war through gifts for major projects across the country such as our own MacRobert Hall (opened officially by Lady MacRobert accompanied by her son Sir Alasdair in 1931) she devoted the rest of her life to a series of charitable trusts. There have been many beneficiaries over the years, ranging from Stirling University to the Earl Haig Fund, education, science and technology, conservation and disabled people, along with many projects to benefit the local community. The two main houses on the estate are used for charitable purposes. Alastrean House (the name derived from the Christian names of the three MacRobert sons) was for many years a retirement home for ex-service personnel and operated through the R.A.F. Benevolent Fund. The Fund continues to sponsor a number of residents through the present operator, the Balhousie Care Group. The main house, Douneside House, is used as a conference centre during the winter months and as a guest house for Armed Forces personnel and their families at other times. Rates are heavily discounted and there is an excellent leisure centre in addition to residential facilities. The most moving room in the house is the original family library, where the visitor can browse through family photograph albums from before the war which show the MacRobert boys at work and at play.

Cadets from St Andrew's College, Ontario, have joined R.G.C. C.C.F. cadets on Summer Camp at Warcop and Barry Buddon since 2005. Young people of both schools have benefited from this experience, and it is hoped the link may lead to visits by our cadets to Canada in future years, with the prospect of adventurous training activities and cultural visits there.

Cadets visited central London in October 2005, spending the week living on the Cruiser H.M.S. *Belfast*, moored on the Thames. The ship was in service throughout the Second World War and played a leading role in the destruction of the battle cruiser *Scharnhorst*. Later, the ship was active in the Normandy Landings off *Gold* and *Juno* beaches. Following decommissioning from the Royal Navy in 1965, she was saved for the nation in 1971, and remains open to visitors through the Imperial War Museum. Major military and war museums were visited during the trip. The week was particularly interesting and worthwhile, with the novelty of the accommodation making up for the lack of modern conveniences!

Regular visits are paid by Lt Col. A. R. Cram T.D. He has been involved with the unit over a considerable period of time (having for example visited the 1986 Orkney camp), and we were delighted when he accepted our invitation to act in the capacity of Honorary Colonel of the unit in 2005. His experience (he talks of sixty years service and having worn Army, Navy and Observer Corps during that time) and sound advice are invaluable, and he takes a keen and very genuine interest in the progress of individual cadets, regardless of their long-term military commitment. His very fine "Colonel's Quaich" is awarded to an individual or individuals making an outstanding contribution to the C.C.F. in the course of a session.

C.C.F. cadets participated in a major military parade on Union St on 28th June 2008. The aim of the parade was to celebrate the contribution made to society by veterans both during and after their period of military service. It was also hoped the event would present the Army to the community in a way which would emphasise teamwork and skills by espousing the Army's values and standards. Massed Pipes and drums led the procession. The Gordon Highlanders Museum were involved and a fly past by a Nimrod aircraft from R.A.F. Kinloss was planned. Cadets departed for their Summer Camp at Barry Buddon immediately after the event and they saw the parade as a fitting start to their week.

Our Annual Dinner is another tradition which is growing year on year. This is an opportunity to meet those who have been involved with the C.C.F. over many years, and to thank formally the many organizations which provide assistance. Perhaps more significantly, it is an opportunity to say goodbye to S6 cadets who have been with the C.C.F. for five years. The event provides these cadets with an introduction to the protocol of a formal dinner in a military establishment, and marks the end of their time with us as they look back on their achievements and prepare to embark upon the next steps of their careers.

Chapter Fourteen

CONCLUSION

Since the end of National Service the vast majority of young people have had no direct experience of military matters, and have no family members who have served in the Armed Forces. It is not expected that large numbers of cadets will go on to follow military careers (although many will later join one of the university units, with no fewer than six involved in the University of Aberdeen Remembrance Service in 2006). The C.C.F. nevertheless continues to be highly thought of by parents and pupils and the unit makes what Jack Webster calls in *The Auld Hoose* "a vibrant contribution to the life of Gordon's College in the twenty-first century" (p.356). One in five or one in six of our senior school pupils will participate for a year or more, and rewards for longer service are considerable, whether measured in terms of promotion or opportunities for extensive leadership experience, confidence building and teamwork. In addition to military qualifications, many aspects of C.C.F. training combine with preparation for other awards such as the Duke of Edinburgh's Award.

Many schools have difficulty in finding suitable teachers to serve in the C.C.F. Some teachers are nevertheless willing to take on these tasks, with a few having been members of University Officer Training Corps or Air Squadron units. In recent years we have been extremely fortunate. In spring 2008 four Army Section and four R.A.F. Section officers were on the strength. We were joined in August 2007 by W.O.1 James Neilson as School Staff Instructor. Following retirement from his position of Regimental Sergeant Major with the Parachute Regiment (including service in the Falklands) and several years as Overseas Security Manager with the Foreign and Commonwealth Office in British embassies worldwide including Riyadh, Jim is ideally suited to the task of ensuring the smooth administration of the unit and we look forward to the contribution he will make. With the exception of Lt Kirsten Hastie, it has not been easy to recruit female officers since the days of Margaret Ramsay and Margaret Houlihan. We are, however, extremely fortunate in having a team of female teaching colleagues, Miss Wendy MacGregor (Biology), Miss Donna Ellis (Mathematics) and Dr Sandra Lonie (Physics), on whom we regularly call to provide female supervision. This allows our many able and enthusiastic female cadets to participate in the full range of activities. We are very grateful to these ladies.

One further illustration of the value placed by the College on military training and experience lies in our official status as a "supportive employer". Along with representatives from employers such as BP, Grampian Police and many small North East businesses, the Head of College and Contingent Commander were presented with a certificate signed by Secretary of State for Defence Geoff Hoon at a ceremony in the Gordon Highlanders Museum in 2005. This certificate, issued though SaBRE (Support for Britain's Reservists and Employers), recognizes that the College actively supports the membership of employees in branches of the Reserve Forces in the knowledge that the commitment of the College to enable such membership in terms of finance and time is more than repaid through the training, personal development and management experience gained by these employees. This support goes beyond current members of the C.C.F. and includes for example Head Janitor and Territorial Army Staff Sgt Kevin Burnett of 51 Sqn, 32 Signals Regiment.

As stated, the C.C.F. is directly controlled by the Ministry of Defence, which demands high standards of efficiency. Biennial Reviews are held and the units (and individuals) come under the scrutiny of high-ranking officers. Over the years our inspection reports have been consistently good, as confirmed by a selection of comments:

> This is a thriving, well led and motivated voluntary contingent, who produced a spirited parade and comprehensive selection of training activities.
>
> *Lt General Sir Alexander Boswell K.C.B., C.B.E., General Officer Commanding The Army in Scotland* July 1983.

> I congratulate the new Contingent Commander, Capt. Bruce Simms, on running a first-class Contingent.
>
> *Col. A. G. Ross, O.B.E., Chief of Staff H.Q. Scotland* October 1990.

> Staff are to be congratulated on their excellent leadership and organisational skills. To a person, everyone seemed happy to be there. It was a lively, thriving contingent. The contingent has every reason to be proud of what it has achieved. I relished my day with them.
>
> *Lt Col. K. M. Potts, SCOTS, SO1 Operations HQNI* 2006.

The term "voluntary contingent" as used above is an important one. C.C.F. membership in many independent schools is compulsory for at least part of the school career of all pupils. It is a matter of pride that all successes of our pupils and staff have been achieved in a contingent where membership is entirely voluntary.

The unit has received tremendous backing from a variety of sources over the years. In particular, we are extremely grateful to the Reserve Forces and Cadets Association (formerly the Territorial and Volunteer Reserve Forces Association), 21 Cadet Training Team, 51 (Scottish) Brigade, the Joint Cadet Secretariat, Headquarters Air Cadets, R.A.F. Cranwell, the C.C.F. R.A.F.

Training, Evaluation and Support Team (Scotland) and many local units including 12 Air Experience Flight R.A.F. Leuchars, 622 Volunteer Gliding School, R.M. Condor Arbroath and staff at Gordon Barracks, Bridge of Don.

Thanks are also due to all College C.C.F. officers past and present who have given so much of their time and energy to the organization. Without the willing support and enthusiasm of so many adults over the sixty years of the C.C.F. and 100 years of involvement of College pupils in military activities, none of the very many achievements listed here would have been possible. It can be stated with confidence that the very many former cadets would wish to acknowledge the tremendous debt of gratitude they owe to these officers.

The College has a proud tradition of service. Qualities encouraged and developed by the C.C.F. are greatly in demand in all walks of life, and we remain confident that future pupils will derive great benefit from membership of the organisation and participation in the many activities offered. Along with our teaching colleagues who provide education in its widest sense to all our pupils, training provided by the C.C.F. unit aims to increase the awareness of our military tradition. Our pupils are encouraged to reflect on the nature of society today. They are encouraged to be willing to serve and not, as many would have us believe of the young people of today, wish simply to be served.

APPENDICES

PART TWO

APPENDIX A

COMMANDING OFFICERS, R.G.C. CADET UNITS

Flt. Lt. R M MacAndrew	1941	A.T.C.
Flt. Lt. J Geals	1943	A.T.C.
Major R R Stewart	1942	A.C.F.
Capt. A S Fraser	1944	A.C.F.
Major J B Hugelshover	1945	A.C.F.
Major R P Mowat	1946	A.C.F.
Major M M MacRae	1948	C.C.F.
Capt. O W McLauchlan	1952	C.C.F.
Capt. R D Gill	1953	C.C.F.
Capt. B Ludwig	1955	C.C.F.
Capt. T Collins	1957	C.C.F.
Major J G Dow	1960	C.C.F.
Major B B Simms	1988	C.C.F.
Sqn Ldr D W Montgomery	1997	C.C.F.

APPENDIX B

HONOURS AND APPOINTMENTS

This list is undoubtedly incomplete. We would welcome further information from Gordonians or their families.

M.B.E.

(for services to the Cadet Forces)
Major John Dow

Cadet Forces Medal

Major John Dow
Capt. John Gordon
Capt. Tom Collins
Major Bruce Simms
Major Kevin Cowie
Capt. Andrew Hopps
Flt. Lt. Harvey Pole
Capt. Michael Maitland
Sqn. Ldr. Daniel Montgomery

Lord Lieutenant's Commendation

Major K S Cowie
Flt. Lt. Harvey Pole
Flt. Lt. Margaret Houlihan
Capt. Michael Maitland
Capt. David Morris

Commandant Air Cadets' Commendation

Sqn. Ldr. Daniel Montgomery

Lord Lieutenant's Cadet

C.S.M. Austin Muller	1989
Col. Sgt. Neil Cargill	1998
Sgt. Claire Hopkins	2001
Sgt. Isabel Wreford	2002
C.W.O. Thomas Hansford	2004
Col. Sgt. Fraser Maitland	2005
Col. Sgt. Sarah Beaton	2006
Sgt. Timothy Thornton	2007
Col. Sgt. Christopher Gray	2008

APPENDIX C

PIPE BAND APPOINTMENTS

Pipe Majors

Kenny Melvin
Walter Anderson
Ian Smith
KiKi Whyte
Jimmy (Sammy) Bain
Robbie Allan
Bill Fraser
Frank Phillip   1970 – 72
Graham Brown   1972 – 73
Robert Sutherland   1973 – 76
Hector Sutherland   1976 – 78
David Smylie   1978 – 80
Ramsay Urquhart   1981 – 83
James Sutherland   1984 – 85
Andrew Sinclair   1985 – 87
Tony Byrne   1987 – 88
Thor Garden   1989 – 91
Michael Ritchie   1991 – 93

Pipe Majors, Drum Majors, Leading Drummers & Staff (under Capt. Michael Maitland) 1993 – 2008

Pipe Major		Leading Drummer	
Date	**Name**	**Date**	**Name**
1993 – 95	Paul Ritchie	1992 – 94	Xander Kuperij
1995 – 97	Christopher Levings	1994 – 95	Philip Booth
1997	Alasdair Smith	1995 – 97	Duncan Rhodes
1997 – 98	Duncan Watson/		
	Robert Duke	1997 – 98	Mark Trimmer
1998 – 99	Steven Esson	1998 – 99	Lucy Rennie
1999 – 2000	Andrew MacMillan	1999 – 2001	Steven Craig
2000 – 01	Duncan Grassie		
2001 – 02	Thomas Fraser	2001 – 02	Neil Johnstone
2002 – 04	Andrew Black	2002 – 05	Eileen Mutch
2004 – 05	Scott Shepherd		
2005 – 06	Fraser Maitland	2005 – 06	Iain Munro
2006 – 07	Ian Christie	2006 – 07	Chris Henderson
2007 – 08	Ewan Robertson	2007 – 08	Ellis Lawrie

Drum Major

1992 – 94	Steven Jenkins
1994 – 95	Robbie Kennedy
2007 –	Conner Hamilton

Piping Instructor		Drumming Instructor	
Date	**Name**	**Date**	**Name**
1993 –	Mr M Maitland	– 96	Mrs L Greenwell
		1996 – 99	Mr G Forbes
		2002 – 04	Mr A Stott
		2005 –	Miss E Mutch

APPENDIX D

C.C.F. PRIZES AWARDED ANNUALLY WITH 2008 RECIPIENTS

NAME OF TROPHY	RECIPIENT
Best Advanced Cadet	L. Cpl Jonathan Mann
Best A.P.C.	Cdt. Charlie Ross and
Donated by Major K.S. Cowie	Cdt. Sean Greaves
Best Shot	L. Cpl. Tom Murdoch
Best Overall	Sgt. Christopher Gray
Donated by Mr. B.R.W. Lockhart	
Best Recruit	Cdt. Bethany Saul
Best Army Cadet Annual Camp –	Sgt. Angus Coull
Dargai Quaich	

R.A.F. Section

Most Promising Recruit	Cdt. Marcus Rose
Donated by Flt Lt G. House	
Best Cadet	C.W.O. Tim Thornton
Donated by Mr G. Allan	
Best Contribution	Cpl. David Smith
Donated by Mrs R. Livingstone	
Best Shot	Cpl. Thomas Raeburn

Joint

Colonel's Quaich	Army Section Scottish Schools
Donated by Lt. Col. A.R. Cram T.D.	C.C.F. Military Skills
	Competition team
Initiative Award	Sgt. Liam McNeil
Donated by Mr A. Urquhart	

APPENDIX E

FORMER CADETS AND ATTENDANCE AT CAMPS

1974 Annual Camp – Orkney

July

Officers
John G Dow (Maj.)
Tom Collins (Capt.)
John Y Gordon (Capt.)

Cadets

Robertson G D
Ewen W S
MacDonald M L
Reid M J M
Gray C G D
Short A
Armstrong D A
McKenzie B M
Sutherland R
Barclay C J
Everett C J
Frieslich C J
Henderson J G
King G
MacFarlane J P A
Milne A E N
Pocock F A
Walker A
Scott-Brown A W
Steele W R
Young G A
Gauld R
Smith N P
Stephen N
Walker I
Goldie P D
Ollason
Mitchell
Thomson

Topps D A
Lewis P M
Ritchie G A
Reid N J N
Gray W N
Johnston R F
Hay B A
MacMillan G C
Sinclair R C
Drew S L K
Findlater P J
Guthrie A J
Johnston K J
Laing C D
McLennan I C
Munro H W
Robertson A R
Webster A
Youngson G D
West J S
Williamson D A R
Low M
Sutherland H
Pratt P L

1986 Annual Camp – Cultybraggan

Dec

Officers	Cadets	
John G Dow (Maj.)	Douglas Alan (C.S.M.)	Williams Nicholas
Bruce B Simms (Capt.)	Pepper Alan (C.Q.M.S.)	Shirreffs George
Kevin S Cowie (Lt.)	Humphries Cameron (Cpl)	Hill Craig (absent)
Andrew L Hopps (Lt.)	Coutts Ronnie (Cpl)	Garden Thor
	Birt James (Cpl)	McAra Andrew
	Duncan Henry (Cpl)	Hall David
	Vermeulen John (Cpl)	Daniels Jamie
	Allan Edward (Cpl)	Cowie Simon
	Shearer George (Cpl)	Fraser Bruce
	Harvey Kevin (Cpl)	Neilson Derek
	Cuthbert Neil (L. Cpl)	Clark Stuart
	Craig Eric (L. Cpl)	Bain Christopher
	Winning Scott (L. Cpl)	Metson Nicholas
	Mitchell Ross (L. Cpl)	Whitehead Simon
	HendersonRichard (L. Cpl)	Bremner Ronald
	Salah-Uddin Hanif (L. Cpl)	Cowie Richard
	Rendall Erland (L. Cpl)	Limet Michael
	Murphy John (L. Cpl)	Thornton Jeremy
	Knaggs Marcus (L. Cpl)	Blair
	Morrice Chris (L. Cpl)	Grant Stephen
	Tunrbull Damien (L. Cpl)	Maitland Stephen
	McAra Alan (L. Cpl)	Adie Charles
	Longhurst Simon	Livingstone Duncan
	Hulme Russell	Wilkie Greg
	Phillips Tilo	Sheves Andrew
	Main Cameron (absent)	Muller Austin
	Campbel Alistair	Cochrane Michael
	Webb Andrew	Hastie
	Bremner Stewart	Garden Mark
	Beaton Scott	Woodhouse Richard
	Fraser Simon	Sutherland Gordon
	Smith Colin	Hung Wiliam
	Garioch Graeme	Nicol Steven
	Sangster Alan	Mackenzie Richard
	Williamson Jonathan	Pickels Christopher
	Sutherland John	Hunt Robert
	Aitkenhead Neil	Whelan Tristan
	Swanson Calum	Duckworth Nicholas

1988 Annual Camp – Warcop

July

Officers	Cadets	
John G Dow (Maj.)	Harvey Kevin C.S.M. S6	Wildgoose Fraser **S2**
Bruce B Simms (Capt.)	Sangster A (Sgt) **S5**	Lindsay Scott
Kevin S Cowie (Lt)	Knaggs Marcus (Sgt)	Costin William
Andrew L Hopps (Lt)	Duckworth Nicholas Sgt	Elrick B
	Mitchell Ross (Sgt)	Duguid A
	Winning Scott (Sgt)	McFadden G
	Neilson Derek (L. Cpl) **S4**	Lamb L
	Baghurst Alasdair	Pike Jonathan
	Fraser S	Zee C
	McAra A (Cpl)	McArthur S
	Hall David	Purnell B
	Garden Thor (Cpl)	Kerridge B
	Bremner Ronald (L. Cpl)	Keilloch D
	Sheves Andrew (Cpl)	Mason S
	Garioch Graeme (Cpl)	Cruden Graeme
	Bremner Stewart (L. Cpl)	Kane Simon
	Campbell Alastair (L. Cpl)	Bayman Tim
	Webb Andrew (Cpl)	Johnston S
	Aitkenhead Neil (L. Cpl)	Cooper P
	Phillips Tilo	Marr Rogan
	Williamson Jon (L. Cpl)	Sheves Iain
	Livingstone Duncan(Cpl)	Brims C
	Williams Nicholas (L. Cpl)	Russell Peter
	Muller Austin (Sgt)	Lumsden Colin
	Cochrane Michael (L. Cpl)	
	Smith Colin (L. Cpl)	Wilkie Greg
	Nicol Steven **S3**	Garden Mark
	Adie Charles	Grant S
	MacKenzie Robert	Nilssen Kristain S2
	Woodhouse Richard	Coates M
	Clark Stuart	Reid Andrew
	Gemmell Mark	Reilly Chris
	Pickles Christopher	
	Thornton Jeremy	
	Bain Christopher	

1991 Nominal Roll

Mar

Officers
Bruce B Simms (Maj.)
Kevin S Cowie (Capt.)
Andrew L Hopps (Capt.)

Cadets
Borowski Mark **S4**
Crouch John
Erskine Grant
Gair Neil
Lind William
MacNaugthon Murray
Pocock James
Ballantyne Neil
Campbell Robert
Douglas Steven
Goodacre Andrew
Walker L
Auld Steven
Benzie Ralph
Fraser David

Brennan M **S3**
Casher Edward
Corpe Lee
Corr Daniel
Costin John
Cruickshank L
Dailly Chris
Dailly Matthew
Fowler J
Jack Chris
Jones Marc
Kirkvleut S
Miller Andrew
Clark C
Pickup Duncan
Polson R
Raimondo Bruce
Rapley Michael
Robertson Raymond
Rose Andrew
Sayers Gary
Cooper Jeremy

Cadets
Sloan David **S2**
Krukowski Esther
Young J
O'Connor Katherine
Anderson Emma
Cunningham C
Coutts A
Sangster M
Willis Dawn
Hill Amy
Duncan K
Chisholm Elliot
Leheny Ian
Jenkins Steven
Kilminster David
Stanbridge Chris
Mitchell Gregor
Fleming A
Insh Ailsa
Munro B
Hay Austin
Forbes Gareth
Fearn Chris
Thomas J
Adams I
Chalmers D
Grant I
Whyte Barry
Liva Anthony
Matheson Ian
Miller Andrew
Davis Jamie
Stephenson T
Ramsay E
Paterson C
Daly Thomas
Disotto Kevin
Grimes Andrew
Mann Graeme
Duthie R

Year	Cadet Sergeant Major (Most Senior Army Cadet)
83 – 84	Dougal Morgan
84 – 85	Blair Estep
85 – 86	X Barclay
86 – 87	Alan Douglas
87 – 88	Harvey Kevin
88 – 90	Nicholas Duckworth
89 – 90	Austin Muller
90 – 91	Greg Wilkie
91 – 92	Andrew Reid
92 – 93	James Pocock
93 – 94	Christopher Jack
94 – 95	Steven Jenkins

APPENDIX F

NOMINAL ROLL
ON 1ST OCTOBER 2007

R. A. F Section

Thornton	Tim	Flt Sgt
Adam	Robert	Sgt
McNeil	Liam	Sgt
Jones	Greg	Sgt
Raeburn	Thomas	Cpl
Gordon	Nick	Cpl
McGregor	Mhairi	Cpl
Sumner	Mary	Cpl
Smith	David	J. Cpl
Johnston	John	J. Cpl
Banks	Adam	Cdt
Bowen	Glenn	Cdt
Burnside	Harry	Cdt
Dickie	Jasmine	Cdt
Gamblen	Ross	Cdt
Hughes	Michael	Cdt
Jewell	Andrew	Cdt
McClean	Jess	Cdt
McLachlan	Natasha-Leigh	Cdt
Moir	Ross	Cdt
Peacock	Alex	Cdt
Pethick	David	Cdt
Polanski	John	Cdt
Robertson	Corrie	Cdt
Russell	James	Cdt
Steedman	Laura	Cdt

Sumner	Jenny	Cdt
Taylor	Ollie	Cdt
Thomson	Hamish	Cdt
Tsang	Gavin	Cdt
Wood	Emma	Cdt
Anderson	Harris	recruit
Anderson	Scott	recruit
Borwell	Jessica	recruit
Coates	Scott	recruit
Copland	Fionnlagh	recruit
De Lecq	Simon	recruit
James	Caroline	recruit
MacAskill	Jordan	recruit
McDougall	Aleks	recruit
Marguerie	Rene	recruit
May	Jonathan	recruit
Nohwaica	Anna	recruit
Nohwaica	Michal	recruit
O' Donnell	Cian	recruit
Rose	Marcus	recruit
Scott	Katherine	recruit
Stanyer	Rory	recruit
Wright	Jonathan	recruit

Army Section

		Year
Abbot	Jack	3
Ashcroft	Calum	2
Atevenson	Alexander	2
Banks	Oliver	2
Bartlett	Thomas	2
Baxter	Mariella	2
Bayliss	Abigail	2
Birnie	Sean	2

Blake	Douglas	6
Bonner	Rory	3
Brooks	Conor	2
Bruce	Eilidh	2
Buchan	Corey	6
Burrows	Caroline	6
Campion	Daniel	2
Chadaga	Rahul	3
Clarkson	David	2
Collins	Liam	2
Collinson	Aidan	2
Compatangelo	Angelica	3
Coull	Angus	5
Craig	Rebecca	2
Davidson	Rebecca	3
Deist	Joni	2
Donaldson	Sarah	4
Dunbar	Robert	3
Duncan	William	3
Fisher	Emma	2
Flanagan	Ronan	3
Gilbert	James	2
Gomersall	Tim	4
Grant	Chris	3
Grant	Michael	4
Gray	Cameron	2
Gray	Christopher	5
Greaves	Mark	2
Greaves	Sean	3
Gurney	Thomas	3
Hamilton	Emma	6
Harris	Cameron	2
Helmore	Joseph	2
Hopps	Erin	3
Horn	Murray	2
Hunter	Alexandar	2
Jefferyes	Zoifa	3
Johnston	Matthew	2

Lord Lieutenant's Cadet Sgt. Isabel Wreford with Lord Lieutenant Margaret Smith Autumn 2002

Flt. Sgt. Thomas Hansford with H.R.H. The Prince of Wales and Lord Lieutenant John Reynolds at the Gordon Highlanders Museum 2005
Photograph: Doug Westland

Flt. Sgt. Thomas Hansford with Lord Lieutenant John Reynolds Autumn 2004.
Photograph: Aberdeen City Council

Thomas with the Sir John Thomson Memorial Sword, R.A.F. Cranwell, July 2005

Presentation of the Sir John Thomson Memorial Sword for Best C.C.F. R.A.F. Cadet in the U.K. 2005
Left to right Flt. Lt. Neil Johnson, Sqn. Ldr. Daniel Montgomery, C.W.O. Thomas Hansford, Mrs. Denise
Hansford, Mr. Hugh Ouston, Flt. Lt. Greg House

C.W.O. Thomas Hansford (second right) at
R.A.F. Linton-on-Ouse with Gordonians (Left
to right) Lt. Cdr. Pete Lumsden, Flt. Lt. Anton
Wisely and Flt. Lt. Greg House

Col. Sgt. Sarah Beaton with H.R.H. The Princess Royal,
November 2006
Photograph: Aberdeen City Council

Col. Sgt. Sarah Beaton with Lord Lieutenant
John Reynolds. Autumn 2006.
Photograph: Aberdeen City Council

Presentation of Lord Lieutenant's badge and certificate to Col. Sgt. Fraser Maitland in the Governors' Room 2005. Left to right Mr. A. Doe, Sqn. Ldr. B. Donald (R.F.C.A.), Rev. D. Smart, Lt. D. Morris, Mrs. E. Doe, Lt. Col. A.R. Cram T.D., Sqn. Ldr. D.W. Montgomery, Dr. S. Lonie, Lord Lieutenant John Reynolds, Sgt. Maj. Clempson (21 C.T.T.), Mr. P. Skingley, Miss W. MacGregor, Mrs. J. Montgomery, Mr. W. Maitland, P.O. D Carnegie, Flt. Lt. N. Johnson, P.O. R. Wakeford, Col. Sgt. F. Maitland, Capt. C. Spracklin, Maj. J. Dow M.B.E., Maj. K. Cowie, Lt. M. Maitland, Sgt. I. Munro, Mr. R. Duncan, Mrs. P. Maitland, Mr. M. Elder, Flt. Sgt. P. Frampton, Mr. H. Ouston, Mrs. A. Everest.
Photograph: Aberdeen City Council

R.A.F. Section National Ground Training Competition Scottish Champions at RAF Uxbridge January 2007 Left to right: John Johnston, Nicholas Gordon, Rachel Meldrum, Tim Thornton, Mary Sumner, Hannah Reid, Thomas Raeburn, Leanne Duff, Andy Gordon, Robert Adam, Mhairi McGregor, Gregory Jones, Liam McNeil, Sqn. Ldr. Daniel Montgomery

Above: Wg. Cdr. G. Clayton-Jones, H.Q. Air Cadets R.A.F. Cranwell, presents Sqn. Ldr. D.W. Montgomery with the Commandant Air Cadets Certificate of Meritorious Service, Nov. 2007

Lt. Col. A.R. Cram T.D. presents the Colonel's Quaich for the first time to Col. Sgt. Fraser Maitland

Successful senior cadets summer 2007: Sgt. Timothy Thornton, Sgt. Innes Worsman, Sgt. Liam McNeil

Successful 2007 Wapinschaw shooting teams:
Left to right: Caroline Burrows, Kirsty Sneddon, John Johnston, Louis Kinsey, Nicholas Gordon, Andy Gordon, Sarah Beaton, Robert Adam, Thomas Raeburn, Christopher Gray, Liam McNeil, Mhairi McGregor

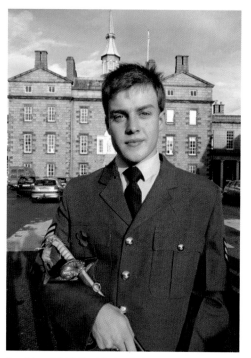

Sgt. Liam McNeil with the Cubby Sword for Best Cadet of the 2007 Air Cadet Leadership Course, R.A.F. Cranwell

Winner of Individual Cadet shooting competition Cpl. Kirsty Sneddon, Wapinschaw 2007

Senior cadets who successful completed the national Cadet Leadership Course at Nesscliff, Shropshire, Easter 2008: Cpl. Thomas Rust, Cpl. Chris Gray, Cpl. Ross MacFarlan, Cpl. Tamzyn Mathers and Cpl. Angus Coull

Flt. Sgt. Timothy Thornton receiving his Lord Lieutenant's Cadet badge and certificate from Lord Provost Peter Stephen, 8th October 2007

2008 Wapinschaw teams:
Front row left to right: Cpl. Ami Munro, Sgt. Tamzyn Mathers, L.Cpl. Thomas Murdoch, Sgt. Chris Gray, Sgt. Angus Coull
Rear row left to right: Cpl. Kirsty Sneddon, Clr. Sgt. Caroline Burrows, Clr. Sgt. Craig Melton, C.S.M. Calum Nixon, Sgt. Jason Rudd, Sgt. Thomas Rust, Sgt. Ross MacFarlan

S6 cadets 2007-08 who have completed 5 years successful service pictured with Col. A.K. Miller C.B.E., Chief Executive, Highland Reserve Forces and Cadets Association:
Front row: Flt. Sgt. Tim Thornton, C.S.M. Calum Nixon, Sqn. Ldr. Montgomery, Col. Miller, Sgt. Robert Adam, Cpl. Kirsty Sneddon
Middle row: Clr. Sgt. Caroline Burrows, Clr. Sgt. Sam Thomas, Cpl. Mary Sumner, Clr. Sgt. Corey Buchan, J/ Cpl John Polanski
Rear row: Clr. Sgt. Malcolm Wright, Clr. Sgt. Craig Melton, Clr. Sgt. Jason Rudd, Clr. Sgt. Innes Worsman
Absent: Clr. Sgt. Emma Hamilton, Cpl. Andrew Krahn

Cadets with staff aboard H.M.Y. Britannia (whilst still in service)
in Aberdeen Harbour 1997

Wessex helicopter in Front Quad 3rd March1966
Photograph: Aberdeen Journals Ltd

Prize winners 2008 with Croup Captain Malcolm Evans M.Ed., Chief of Staff Air Cadets, inspecting officer at the 2008 Biennial Review:
Left to right: Cpl. David Smith, Cdt. Sean Greaves, Cdt. Charlie Ross, Cdt. Bethany Saul, C.W.O. Tim Thornton, Sgt. Liam McNeil, Group Captain Evans, Cpl. Thomas Raeburn, Col. Sgt. Craig Melton, Sgt. Angus Coull, Sgt. Christopher Gray, L. Cpl. Thomas Murdoch, Cdt. Marcus Rose
Absent: L. Cpl. Jonathan Mann

Lord Provost John Reynolds and senior cadets meet residents at the Erskine Hospital unit, Bridge of Don 2004

Flt. Sgt. Peter Frampton Lays a poppy on the grave of Sgt. Andrew Caie in Allenvale Cemetery Aberdeen. Sgt. Caie was College Junior Sports Champion in 1936

Crest displayed on "MacRobert's Reply" aircraft of
XV Sqn. 1941-present day
Image courtesy of Squadron Prints Ltd, Arbroath

Grave of Signalman Lawrence A. Davie, killed in
Normandy, 7th June 1944. Bayeux War Cemetery

"MacRobert's Reply" Tornado GR 1 of XV Sqn, R.A.F. Lossiemouth
Image courtesy of Squadron Prints Ltd, Arbroath

Geoffrey deHavilland Flying Foundation Medal winner Cadet Warrant Officer Timothy Thornton with papents Alison and John Thornton at Air Squadron Day, R.A.F. Cranwell June 29th 2008

Lance Corporal Gordon Campbell, Royal Marines
1978 - 2006

Lt. Col. & Mrs A.R. Cram with Sqn. Ldr. D.W. Montgomery on the occasion of the appointment of Lt. Col. Cram as Acting Honorary Colonel, R.G.C. C.C.F.

R.G.C. C.C.F. May 2007

Officers and senior cadets May 2007:
Front Row: 2Lt. K. Hastie, Capt. D. Morris, Capt. M. Maitland, Capt. C. Spracklin, Lt. Col. A.R. Cram T.D., Sqn. Ldr. D.W. Montgomery, Flt. Lt. R. Wakeford, F.O. D. Carnegie, P.O. M. McCrum (not present: Flt. Lt. N. Johnson)
Rear Row: Clr. Sgt. S. Beaton, Clr. Sgt. R. Wood, Clr. Sgt. A. Gao, Cp.l R. Farrell, Clr. Sgt. D. Frost, Clr. Sgt. C. Hawthorne, C.S.M. C. Henderson, Flt. Sgt. A. Gordon, Cdt. L. Peet, Cpl. R. Meldrum, Cpl. L. Duff, Cpl. H. Reid

S6 leavers at the 2007 CCF Annual Dinner:
Front Row: Sarah Beaton, Leanne Duff, Mara Lilley, Iona Naismith, Rachel Meldrum, Alice Rook, Hannah Reid
Rear Row: Ian Christie, Richard Wood, Craig Hawthorne, Robert Farrell, Christopher Henderson, Duncan Frost, Andrew Gordon, Louise Peet

Johnston	Liam	2
Kinsey	Harry	3
Kinsey	Louis	6
Krahn	Andrew	6
Laing	Rory	2
Lasocki	Thaine	2
Lawrie	Ellis	2
Lockhead	Mark	2
MacDonald	Jack	2
MacDonald	Mary	2
Macfarlan	Ross	5
Mackison	Alexander	1
Macvicar	Calum	4
Mann	David	2
Mann	Jonathan	4
Mathers	Tamzyn	5
Mayeux	Hugo	2
McDonald	Kieren	2
McGregor	Fiona	3
McLeod	Kirsty	2
McMillan	Hannah	2
Meldrum	Laura	5
Melton	Craig	6
Milne	Catriona	5
Milne	Matthew	2
Morgan	Andrew	2
Morrell	Scott	2
Munro	Ami	5
Murdoch	Tom	4
Murray	Samantha	2
Nanthakumar	Aran	2
Neilson	Callum	4
Ngu	Samuel	5
Ngu	Sharon	2
Nixon	Calum	6
Notman	Craig	4
Orfali	Lena	3
Ormston	Struan	3

Osman	Fatima	3
Paterson	Alistair	2
Peddie	Grant	2
Robertson	Heather	4
Robertson	Louiise	2
Ross	Charlie	3
Rudd	Jason	6
Rust	Thomas	5
Sandison	Thomas	2
Saul	Betthany	2
Shepherd	Peter	2
Smith Lawrence	Tabiyha	2
Sneddon	Kirsty	6
Sneddon	Robbie	3
Somers	Adele	2
Stevens	Ruth	2
Stevenson	Alexander	2
Strachan	Georgia	3
Strang	Caitlan	2
Tawse	Benjamin	2
Thom	Samuel	2
Thomas	Sam	6
Thompson	Katriona	3
Thomson	Andrew	2
Thomson	Emily	4
Turner	Cameron	2
Wang	Alex	3
Watson	Patrick	2
Whyte	Ruth	4
Wilson	Jamie	3
Wilson	Sebastian	3
Wolsey	Robyn	2
Woodford	Connor	2
Worsman	Innes	6
Wright	Malcolm	6
Yule	James	2
Zhu	Oliver	3

APPENDIX G

AIR SQUADRON DAY, R.A.F. CRANWELL 2008: SELECTED ITEMS FROM PROGRAMME

Foreword by Commandant Air Cadets
Air Commodore Ian Stewart B.Sc (Hons) R.A.F.

Air Squadron Day is an important event in the Combined Cadet Force (R.A.F.) calendar. The awards that will be made today provide an important focus for cadet training throughout the year and I am grateful to the Air Squadron and the Geoffrey de Havilland Flying Foundation for providing these prizes. The following will be presented during this important event: the Air Squadron Trophy for the Best R.A.F. Section; the Sir John Thomson Memorial Sword to the Best C.C.F. (R.A.F.) cadet; and the Geoffrey de Havilland Flying Foundation Medals for C.C.F. achievement.

The Combined Cadet Force is in good shape and continues to be part of an expanding Air Cadet Organisation that will see a planned increase in overall cadet numbers from 42,000 to 50,000 over the next ten years. Involvement in the Combined Cadet Force provides a welcome break from the demands of the academic syllabus and develops young people's powers of leadership through training to promote the qualities of responsibility, self-reliance, resourcefulness, endurance, perseverance and a sense of service to the community.

On parade today you will see shining examples of the excellent young people who have reached the pinnacle of achievement for their age. You will hear details of their individual and team successes from the Secretary of the Air Squadron, Simon Ames. I urge you to engage with all the cadets this afternoon and I know you will not be disappointed with the talents these young people display. They all represent the best of an outstanding organisation.

I hope you enjoy your day.

The Air Squadron

Origins: The Air Squadron was founded in 1966 by a group of friends who shared a passionate interest in flying light aircraft. The founder members were the Hon. Hugh Astor, Air Cdre Sir Peter Vanneck and the Hon. Anthony Cayzer. Two of the earliest members were Second World War heroes Sir Douglas Bader and Sir Hugh Dundas. Others were Sir Max Aitken, Tommy Sopwith and Lord Waterpark.

Constitution: It was decided always to limit the size of the Squadron to 100 active members in order to maintain the original intention of being a group of friends with a common interest in flying. All new members have to hold a pilotage qualification and preferably to own or have a share in an aircraft (fixed wing or rotary).

Support for British Aviation: From the early days, the Air Squadron wished to support the future of British Aviation in various ways and also to forge close links with all three flying Services. To this end the Air Squadron presents annual trophies for Aerobatics and for the best C.C.F. Air Cadet unit in the country. A Sword of Honour in memory of Air Squadron member Air Chief Marshal Sir John Thomson is also given to the best individual Air Cadet at an annual ceremony at R.A.F. Cranwell. Cadets are also given flight experience flying in a range of aircraft belonging to Air Squadron members.

Charity support: The Air Squadron has its own charity, the Geoffrey de Havilland Flying Foundation, which continues to support aviation education and help young people to fulfil their ambition to be able to "reach for the sky".

Overseas Expeditions: Starting with regular trips in the U.K. and to France, the Air Squadron has undertaken ever more ambitious trips overseas often at the invitation of foreign governments or their air forces. These required meticulous planning and daring execution, hallmarked by adventure and good ambassadorship. In the past two decades they have flown their aircraft to Russia, Jordan, Tanzania, Pakistan and Morocco. In 2000, the Air Squadron flew across the North Atlantic in order to tour the length and breadth of the U.S.A. as far west as Alaska. In Washington, a millennium Sword of

Honour was presented to the United States Air Force. The sword is kept in the Pentagon and awarded to the top Air Force cadet each year.

In 2003, the hundredth year of powered flight was commemorated by the Air Squadron flying to Cape Town, a round trip of 16,500 miles. A ceremonial sword was presented to the South African Air Force which is awarded every six months to the top passing-out officer cadet at the Academy. In 2006, members visited Poland, marking the occasion with a Spitfire flypast over Warsaw, a salute to distinguished Polish airmen.

Looking forward: At the start of the new millennium, the Air Squadron continues to embrace the principles of friendship and adventure among dedicated aviators.

Its members represent every facet of British aviation, from military to civil, fixed wing to rotary, war-birds and classic aircraft to home-built.

The Air Squadron Trophy

The Air Squadron Trophy is awarded annually to the Best R.A.F. Section participating in the Air Squadron Trophy Competition. Each of the six C.C.F. areas covering the whole of the U.K. hold an area competition to determine the best two R.A.F. Sections in each area to go forward to the National Final which is held towards the end March of each year at R.A.F. Cranwell. Each team comprises thirteen cadets – a leader plus twelve. The final competition involving twelve R.A.F. Sections and 156 cadets consists of seven elements: First Aid, Shooting, Fitness Test, R.A.F. Knowledge Test, Aircraft Recognition, Drill and a Command Task. The Trophy is awarded on Air Squadron Day, traditionally on either the last Sunday of June or the first Sunday of July each year at a grand occasion at R.A.F. Cranwell. The top three teams are invited to attend and each team leader will receive a Geoffrey de Havilland Flying Foundation Medal for C.C.F.

Achievement: At Cranwell, not only will the winning teams receive their prizes but all cadets will get the chance to fly in aircraft owned by members of the Air Squadron – Tiger Moths, YAKs, de Havilland Rapide, Cessnas, helicopters and many others – an unforgettable experience. This competition provides a welcome focus for all training throughout the year so as many R.A.F. Sections as possible are encouraged to take part.

Sir John Thomson Memorial Sword
for Best C.C.F. (R.A.F.) Cadet 2008
as presented by
Lady Jan Thomson
to
Cadet Warrant Officer Thomas Hansford
Robert Gordan's College
C.C.F. (R.A.F. Section)

The Sir John Thomson Memorial Sword commemorates the late Air Chief Marshal Sir John Thomson G.C.B. C.B.E. A.F.C. R.A.F. who died on 10th July 1994 aged 53. Sir John was a leading member and strong supporter of the Air Squadron and regularly flew cadets on Air Squadron Day and on Air Experience Flights. The Sword is awarded annually to the cadet judged to be the Best in the C.C.F. (R.A.F.). Cadets, who will invariably be the most senior in their Section/Contingent, will have to demonstrate the highest level of C.C.F. commitment and involvement, will have made the most of all opportunities offered to them during their time in the C.C.F. and will also be highly regarded within their School or College. Nominations are called for in November of each year. Of those recommended by either their Contingent Commander or R.A.F. Section Commander, six will be chosen for the final interview with Wing Commander C.C.F. in either late January or early February as a result of which a winner will be chosen. Results are made public in late March and the Sword is awarded at the Air Squadron Day celebrations at the end of the Summer Term. All six finalists, who will attend the parade on Air Squadron Day, will be awarded a Geoffrey de Havilland Flying Foundation Medal for C.C.F. Achievement.

Geoffrey de Havilland Flying Foundation Medals
for Outstanding C.C.F. Achievement 2008
Presented by
Air Marshal Ian Macfadyen
C.B. O.B.E. F.R.AeS
Chairman of the Trustees of de Havilland Flying Foundation
As awarded to Cadet Warrant Officer Timothy Thornton, 2008

APPENDIX H

30TH MARCH 2000
THE CEREMONY OF BEATING RETREAT

Until the nineteenth century armies were reluctant to continue operations after nightfall. The command in the form of a drum signal was given, normally at sunset, to retire to a defensive position, usually a walled town, in order to prevent surprise attack. This also resulted in a close link being established between the closure of the town gates and the lowering of colours at the end of an active day in the field and the term "Beating Retreat".

Early evidence of this can be found in an order dating from 1598.

"Ye Drumme will advertise by beat of drum those required for the Watch."

A similar requirement was still extant in 1727.

"Half an hour before the setting of the sun the drummers of the port guards are to go upon the ramparts and beat a retreat to give notice to those without that the gates are to be shut."

The modern-day ceremony of Beating Retreat takes the form of a musical display and is traditionally held around sunset. This evening the ceremony is re-enacted by Robert Gordon's College C.C.F. Pipe Band.

The Contingent will be inspected by Brigadier S. R. B. Allen, Commander 51st Highland Brigade, who will present the cap badge of The Highlanders to representatives of the Army Section.

APPENDIX I

C.C.F. R.A.F. SECTION ANNUAL CAMPS
1994 - 2008

1994	RAF St. Athan
1995	RAF Cosford
1996	RAF Coltishall
1997	RAF Conningsby
	RAF Honnington
1998	RAF Buchan
	RAF Lyneham
1999	RAF Kinloss
	RAF Cultybraggan
2000	RAF St. Athan
	RAF Wittering
2001	RAF Uxbridge
	RAF Lossiemouth
2002	RAF Sealand
	RAF Northolt
2003	RAF Cosford
	RAF Cranwell
2004	RAF Halton
	RAF Lossiemouth
2005	RAF Uxbridge
	RAF Leuchars
	RAF Brampton
	RAF Rheindhalen
	RAF Akrotiri
2006	RAF Halton
	RAF Linton-on-Ouse
	RAF Akrotiri
	RAF Valley
2007	RAF St. Athan
	RAF Rheindhalen
	RAF Linton-on-Ouse
2008	RAF Cosford
	RAF Akrotiri
	RAF Odiham

ABBREVIATIONS –
MILITARY AND GENERAL

A.C.F.	Army Cadet Force
A.D.C.C.	Air Defence Cadet Corps
A.E.F.	Air Experience Flying
A.T.C.	Air Training Corps
and Bar	Indicates the second award of a medal
B.N.C.A.	British National Cadet Association
C.B.	Companion of the Order of the Bath
C.B.E.	Commander of the Order of the British Empire
C.C.F.	Combined Cadet Force
C.M.G.	Companion of the Order of St. Michael and St. George
C.T.T.	Cadet Training Team
D.C.M.	Distinguished Conduct Medal
D.F.C.	Distinguished Flying Cross
D.F.M.	Distinguished Flying Medal
D.S.C.	Distinguished Servive Cross
D.S.O.	Distinguished Service Order
H.M.S.	Her Majesty's Ship
H.M.Y.	Her Majesty's Yacht
H.Q.	Headquarters
K.C.B.	Knight Commander of the Order of the Bath
M.B.E.	Member of the Order of the British Empire
M.C.	Military Cross
M.M.	Military Medal
M.O.D.	Ministry of Defence
N.C.O.	Non Commissioned Officer

N.G.T.C.	National Ground Training Competition
O.B.E.	Officer of the Order of the British Empire
O.C.	Officer Commanding
O.T.C	Officers' Training Corps
P.o.W.	Prisoner of War
Q.F.I.	Qualified Flying Instructor
R.A.F.	Royal Air Force
R.A.M.C	Royal Army Medical Corps
R.E.M.E.	Royal Mechanical and Electrical Engineers
R.F.C.A.	Reserve Forces and Cadets Association
R.M.	Royal Marines
R.N.	Royal Navy
R.N.R.	Royal Naval Reserve
S.a.B.R.E.	Support for Britain's Reservists and Employers
S.S.	Sister Ship
Sqn	Squadron
T.A.	Territorial Army
T.A.V.R.A	Territorial and Volunteers Reserves Association
T.C.F.	Territorial Cadet Force
T.D.	Territorial Decoration
V.C.	Victoria Cross
V.G.S.	Volunteer Gliding School

RANKS – ARMY SECTION

Cdt.	Cadet
L. Cpl.	Lance Corporal
Cpl.	Corporal
Sgt.	Sergeant
Clr. Sgt.	Colour Sergeant
C.S.M.	Company Sergeant Major
2/Lt.	Second Lieutenant
Lt.	Lieutenant
Capt.	Captain
Maj.	Major
W.O.1	Warrant Officer Class One

RANKS – R.A.F. SECTION

Cdt.	Cadet
J. Cpl.	Junior Corporal
Cpl.	Corporal
Sgt.	Sergeant
Flt. Sgt.	Flight Sergeant
C.W.O.	Cadet Warrant Officer
P.O.	Pilot Officer
F.O.	Flying Officer
Flt. Lt.	Flight Lieutenant
Sqn. Ldr.	Squadron Leader

BIBLIOGRAPHY

Collins, L.J.: *Cadets and the War 1939–45* (Jade Publishing Ltd 2005).

Collins, L.J.: *Cadets –The Impact of War on the Cadet Movement* (Jade Publishing Ltd 2001).

Gunn, A.C.: *The MacRobert Trusts 1943–93* (MacRobert Trusts 1994).

Harris, P.: *Aberdeen and the North East at War* (Lomond Books Ltd 1995).

Lake, D.: *Tartan Air Force* (Birlinn Ltd 2007).

Lockhart, B.: *Robert Gordon's Legacy* (Black & White Publishing Ltd 2007).

Smith, D.J.: *Action Stations No. 7* (Patrick Stephens Ltd 1983).

Webster, J.: *The Auld Hoose* (Black & White Publishing Ltd 2005).

Webster, J.: *A Grain of Truth* (Paul Harris Publishing 1981).

Robert Gordon's College Former Pupils Magazine, various years.

Gordonian, various years.

Minutes of the Quarterly General Court of the Governors and *Meetings of the Secondary School Committee*, various years.

Robert Gordon's College Prospectus, various years.

http://www.rfca.org.uk/rfca_ccf.htm

http://www.cwgc.org

http://www.aircadets.org

http:/www.regiments.org/regiments/U.K./lists/targts.htm

http://www.cambsacf.com

http://www.powysarmycadets.org.U.K./history.cfm

http://www.mod.uk./DefenceInternet/AboutDefence/WhatWeDo/ReserveForcesandCadets/DRFC/HistoryOfTheCombinedCadetForce.htm

http://www.mod.uk./DefenceInternet/AboutDefence/WhatWeDo/ReserveForcesandCadets/DRFC/HistoryOfTheArmyCadetForceACF.htm

http://en.wikipedia.org/wiki/Combined_Cadet_Force

http://www.victoriacross.co.u.k.

http://www.theaward.org

Department of Internal Affairs, Head Office: *Series 898 Archives* (New Zealand/Te Rua Mahara o te K?wanatanga Wellington Office).

INDEX